Forget the Pie!

Forget the Pie!

Recipe for a healthier 401(k)

RIC LAGER

Edited by: JP Payne & Associates, Inc.
Interior graphics by: Woodwind Design & RedJet Media
Cover concept and design, book formatting: RedJet Media.com

I have many lawyers as clients, and I value their opinion as they do mine. I asked a few of them, and they all said the same thing—I have to include the following information in this publication.

The information contained in this book is provided in good faith, and every reasonable effort has been made to ensure that it is accurate and up to date. The ideas and opinions expressed in this book are those of the author. The purpose is to provide helpful and informative material on the subjects expressed herein. The author is not rendering any specific legal, financial or tax advice. If you do require specific professional attention, please consult with a qualified individual who knows your individual situation.

Furthermore, the author is not responsible or liable for any lose that may arise resulting from reliance on any information contained in this book. This also goes for any explanations, opinions, claims, observations, proposed answers, solutions, responses, results, statements, resolutions, retorts, wisecracks or stories arising out of the information contained in this book.

ISBN # 978-1-4243-0912-2

DEDICATION

This book is dedicated to my mother, Gloria H. Lager, who died on April 20, 2005. She taught me to never be afraid, to work hard and to always tell the truth.

ACKNOWLEDGEMENT

I began work as a registered representative in March of 1984. With what I knew about managing my clients' stock market investments at the time, it's a miracle that I lasted in the business until December 1995. Then, I had a life-changing event: I attended my first Dorsey, Wright & Associates seminar.

Tom Dorsey and his staff exposed me to the concept that supply and demand is really what stock market price movement is all about. They shared their philosophy and methodology, and in doing so, provided all the evidence I needed to convince me to "go out on my own."

I promptly made the decision to leave the world of retail brokers and become a registered investment advisor. Thus, my association with Dorsey, Wright & Associates changed my career. And more importantly, it has helped me change the investment careers of my clients.

I only know how to maintain and build a successful registered investment advisory firm using the Dorsey, Wright approach and database. I can't imagine relying on another resource. And in fact, I refuse to do so. I have tried advising clients using the training and tools that everyone else uses in the brokerage business. But Dorsey, Wright & Associates' approach is far superior.

I remain grateful to DWA for my initial and on-going education as an effective and confident advisor. The Dorsey, Wright "Point & Figure Method" of technical analysis is truly essential. Using the DWA approach and market indicators, there is nothing that I can't handle for my clients.

I offer my sincere thanks to my friend Tom Dorsey and his associates, accordingly.

TABLE OF CONTENTS

Chapter One
Why This Book Had To Be Written...1

Chapter Two
Brief History of Point & Figure Analysis...15

Chapter Three
Your Retirement Plan Does Not Work 23

Chapter Four
The Latest Industry Trends Will Not Help 31

Chapter Five
Forget the Pie, You Can Have Your Cake and Eat It, Too.......................................45

Chapter Six
Bullish Percent Concept 53

Chapter Seven
Sector and Asset Class Tools 61

Chapter Eight
Relative Strength 67

Chapter Nine
Relative Strength Examples 77

Chapter Ten
Putting It All Together...81

Chapter Eleven
You Can Have Your Own Investment Policy Statement... 89

Chapter Twelve
How to Give Retirement Plan Advice 99

Chart and Table Examples
How to Give Retirement Plan Advice 115

CHAPTER
one
Why This Book Had To Be Written

I had to write this book. There are over 42 million Americans that are trying desperately to manage their main retirement savings on their own.

Yet when I started writing this book in August of 2005, there was not a single independent and unbiased stock market risk-management tool available that provided specific and timely investment advice on the menu of mutual fund options available to a retirement plan participant.

The problem now, and the problem for the last several stock market cycles, has been that none of the currently offered investment tools engage the retirement plan participant. None of these tools provide the on-going and dynamic information necessary to help a retirement plan investor make the necessary investment management decisions.

This book solves that problem by explaining in detail the application and uses of the stock market risk-management tools that will allow retirement plan participants to make better investment decisions.

In the 24 years since the creation of the 401(k) retirement plan, there has not been one retirement plan advice model created that has benefited the people who have the money in the retirement plan--that is, the retirement plan participants.

In the beginning, retirement plan sponsors offered a retirement plan with investment options picked for them by industry experts. Those "experts" were the financial service firms that offered the retirement plans. Retirement plan participants were simply encouraged to "save as much money as you can for retirement."

Then, retirement plan participants demanded that more options be made available for them to invest in. These participants wanted to take more control of their retirement plans.

Today, with legislation created by the Federal Government and Department of Labor in December of 2001, a retirement plan participant merely has to sign his or her name, and he or she is automatically enrolled in a "suitable" retirement plan option that will adjust the stock and bond holdings based on age, risk tolerance and time until retirement.

In addition, retirement plan participants can hire independent investment advisory firms to manage their retirement plan accounts. Retirement plan participants pay a small fee for a service that analyzes their profile data, runs risk scenarios and estimates their range of expected returns until their retirement.

The same financial "experts" that designed the retirement plan menus that have failed us for 25 years are now telling retirement plan participants that if they have not been able to make any progress in saving for retirement so far, the investment options in the retirement plan will be changed for them. Automatically.

The fact is, the investment results of the current generation of retirement plan participants have been dismal. The case study below will outline just how bad the recent investment returns have been.

Case Study of S&P 500 Returns
Mr. Jones Retirement Plan From 2000-2005

Let's take a look at the reality of the last five years of retirement plan investment returns for a typical retirement plan investor.

Think back 5 years ago. The example below has been a good tool for me with new clients because most of them can remember the "high water mark" of their retirement plan balances in the year-end of 1999.

Below is a picture of the retirement plan situation for Mr. Jones in January 2000. At that time, he was 45 years of age and like the rest of the Baby Boomer Generation, Mr. Jones had definite plans to retire at age 65. With the stock market returns through the year-end of 1999, most retirement plan participants had the same retirement goals.

BEGINNING OF THE YEAR 2000

AGE: 45

EXPECTED RETIREMENT AGE:................................65

RETIREMENT PLAN VALUE:...............................$500,000

EXPECTED ANNUAL RATE OF RETURN:....................11%

AVERAGE ANNUAL CONTRIBUTION:....................$15,000

ANNUAL MUTUAL FUND EXPENSES:....................1.25%

PROJECTED ACCOUNT VALUE AT 65:............$4,000,000

ANNUAL WITHDRAWAL OF 3% AT RETIRE:.......$120,000

I would be the first to sign up for the afore-mentioned $120,000 per year withdrawal in retirement income. I know it is not realistic to think that an 11% annual return is sustainable, but I came up with that annual return number after I surveyed several on-line Retirement Plan Calculator and Retirement Plan Tool Web sites. Every retirement plan provider has these tools. They are found at the same Web site that you use to log in to view your retirement plan account balances. Fidelity, Vanguard, and Bloomberg Web sites all use annual performance returns in the 10-12% range.

Fast-forward five full years of S&P 500 investment returns. The numbers below are not some computer simulation model of what stock market returns are likely to occur. The numbers below are real and the investment returns are in the history books.

<u>Beginning of the Year 2005:</u>

The assumption here is that Mr. Jones' retirement account is 100% invested in the Vanguard 500 Index fund. I use this fund for two reasons. One, it is the largest mutual fund in the world and widely available in many retirement plan menus. Second, this mutual fund is widely considered to be a very efficient and low-cost way to own the S&P 500 Index. Below are the performance numbers of this fund over the five-year period from 1-1-2000 to 12-31-2004.

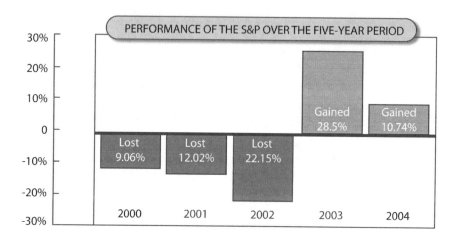

The above numbers add up to performance of -11.36% over the five-year period, or an annual rate of return of -2.38%.

It is an important point here to comment on a couple of major themes I have run into while providing advice to retirement plan investors.

First, the majority of retirement plan participants own mutual fund options in their retirement plan that has a large correlation to the performance of the S&P 500. The average correlation of all US mutual funds performance to the S&P 500 is about .87 according to Morningstar® study at the end of 2003.

I have sat down with many well-intentioned retirement plan participants that were 1/3rd, 1/3rd and 1/3rd invested in three of the mutual fund options in their retirement plan menu. These retirement plan investors thought that they were properly diversified--just like all of the articles they read that told them they should be "diversified".

What this typically turns into for most retirement plan investors is equal investments into two Large Cap Growth mutual funds and a Large Cap Blend mutual fund---probably an investment in the very same S&P 500 index.

The consultants that work with the retirement plan providers are to blame for this mess. Prior to the stock market peak in early 2000, most of the mutual funds available to retirement plan investors were Large Cap funds. That is because for many years in the late 1990's, the best mutual fund options to be invested in were Large Cap Growth funds.

Let me explain. The retirement plan consultants are hired by the retirement plan sponsor to advise them about what mutual fund menu to offer in their company retirement plan. These consultants are required to populate the retirement plan menu with the largest number of choices of the best-performing mutual funds. Thus in early 2000, the investment of choice in the stock market was Large Cap Growth stocks and the mutual funds that owned those stocks.

According to information provided to me by Dorsey, Wright & Associates, Inc., upwards of 75% of all the mutual fund options available to a retirement plan investor are the same kinds of mutual funds----that is, Large Cap Growth. The only difference in most of the mutual fund options available to retirement plan investors is the name of the fund. All Large Cap mutual funds own the same stocks!

This information presents a problem with diversification. It is almost impossible to diversify within any group of mutual funds because of their large correlation of the S&P 500. Even if you own a little bit of International, Small, Mid Cap or even a Bond mutual fund in your retirement plan, you still are looking at very large correlation to the performance of the S&P 500.

Most retirement plan participants choose to invest in mutual fund names they recognize from magazine or television ads. Or they choose mutual funds based on their recent performance. Prior to 2000, Large Cap funds had the best performance of any class of mutual funds and that is where the growth of assets in retirement plans came from. In addition, 65% of all the mutual funds offered to US investors are Large Cap mutual funds.

As you can see, it is very hard to get around the fact that you are investing in an S&P 500 clone in your retirement plan. The mutual fund options may be presented to you with different names and different categories assigned to them, but the performance of these funds follow the performance of the S&P 500 in most cases.

So, if you are like most retirement plan investors right now, you own a large amount of Large Cap Growth mutual funds.

But let's get back to Mr. Jones. Again we fast-forward five years and look at what really happened in regard to the performance of his retirement plan. The annual growth and retirement age assumptions are unchanged. The only things that have changed are the following hard realities:

1. Mr. Jones is now five years older.
2. He has five years less of time to be able to add his own money and his company's matching money to their retirement plan.
3. He is five years closer to retirement.
4. The rate of return on his retirement plan account was close to the annualized performance of the S&P 500.

Age: **50**
Expected Retirement Age: **65**
Account Value: **$518,200**
   (includes $75,000 in contributions)

I want to stop right here, and make this important point. The numbers you see are correct. Mr. Jones began with a $500,000 balance in his retirement plan on 1-1-2000. He did add $75,000 over the 5-year period with the combination of his retirement plan contributions and his employer retirement plan contributions. Assuming his retirement account performed in-line with the returns of the S&P 500, he really does only have $518,200 on 1-1-2005.

So as you see, there was a growth rate of only $3640 per year over the five years, for a total of $18,200. Even with the addition of $75,000 in new money, Mr. Jones had a total investment return of 3.64% over the five-year period, or an annual investment return in his retirement plan of over the five-year period of .73%.

Without the addition of the "new money" to his retirement plan, Mr. Jones was down 26.36% in the value of his retirement plan over those five years. Here is how I arrived at that number: $443,200 minus the $75,000 in new money added to the retirement plan account equals $368,200.

6

If Mr. Jones began 2000 with a $500,000 retirement plan balance, and the account was really worth $368,200 with no new money added, then Mr. Jones actually lost $131,800 on the investments in his retirement plan over the five-year period.

If Mr. Jones had just invested in the money market account option available in his retirement plan for the entire five years, he would at least have had a positive investment return. Even a money market rate of return over the same period of time would have been a positive number.

In the period between 1-1-2000 and 12-31-2004, the investment return on a 13-week Treasury Bill was approximately 13.83%. This rate of return will be a little higher than the return on a money market option in a retirement plan menu, but not by much.

In Mr. Jones' example, his retirement plan value would have been $569,150 on 12-31-2004 if he would have been 100% invested in the money market for the five-year period. That is an annual return of 2.77%.

The Department of Labor requires that a money market, Large Cap stock, Small or Mid Cap stock, International stock and bond option be made available on a basic retirement plan menu of options. You know the investment performance of the Large Cap stock equivalent mutual fund option---that is the S&P 500 Index. And you know the investment performance of the money market account. Here are some other asset class returns over the same five-year time period.

The Morningstar Small Value asset class was up 147% during those five years. The Lehman Brothers Aggregate Bond Index was up 45% during those five years.

As you will see in the chapters eight and nine, the Relative Strength tools can be used to gain the knowledge on how and when to make the necessary asset class decisions and changes in your retirement plan investments.

Now let's finish the rest of this example. From age 50 to his retirement date, here is the really bad news.

Expected Annual Rate of Return:	*11%*
Average Annual Contribution:	*$15,000*
Annual expenses:	*1.25%*
Projected Account Value at 65:	*$2,559,261*
Annual Withdrawal of 3% at Retirement:	*$76,777*

There are three things that should jump out at you here. First, $2,559,261 is a lot less money than $4,000,000. It is 38.98% less to be exact.

Second, take a look at this table below to get an idea of the kind of investment returns necessary to "get back to even" when your retirement plan goes through the kind of principal loss as described in the above example.

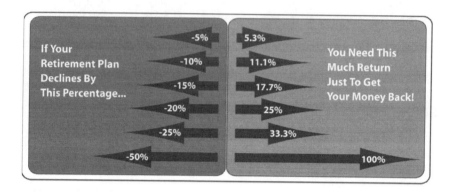

Mr. Jones lost 26.36% of the amount of principal in his retirement account from 2000 to 2005. Here are the steps involved to figure out what type of investment returns are necessary to get his retirement money back to the original amount.

Take the percent loss and divide by (100 minus the percent loss)

> **Investment down by ?% = % return needed to**
> **(100 - % down)   get back to even.**

So, in the case of Mr. Jones, that would be 26.36 divided by 73.64. So the answer is just under 35%. That is the total investment return necessary to get Mr. Jones retirement account "back to even."
Every time I use this calculation with a new client, I am still astonished by the magnitude of the real numbers involved. Even a casual observer of historical stock market returns knows how long it takes to make a 35% return on your investments in the stock market.

Even in a retirement plan account where you have regular contributions from both yourself and your employer every year, and the growth of your account value is free from taxes, it is going to take several years to "get back to even."

Third and I think most important to the way retirement plan investors really think, is the fact that living on $76,777 per year is an entirely different lifestyle than living on $120,000 per year. Even in today's dollars. No matter where you chose to live. What about living on that much less money in future dollars?

In my years of experience in providing investment advice to retirement plan participants at a wide-range of companies and professional organizations, I can tell you that the example used above is far more common than not.

Raising Cash Example

Portfolio A and Portfolio B

In an effort to get all the mathematical examples I use with clients out of the way in the same chapter, let me illustrate to you the story of Portfolio A and Portfolio B. This is one of my favorite stories because it really makes a strong point to new clients about what my retirement plan advisory service is trying to help them do.

I think this is an important example because it illustrates the point that there will be times in the management of your retirement plan account that will call for a larger-than-normal money market balance. As you learn to use and have more confidence in the tools explained in the later chapters of this book, there will come a time in the stock market cycles where you just don't feel comfortable with a large commitment to stock mutual funds and you will have confidence that the safety of the money market is sometimes the best place for your retirement plan assets.

Remember that there are times in the stock market cycle where **Wealth Preservation** is a more important investment objective than **Wealth Accumulation**.

If you have a good stock market memory, think back to about January of 2000. The "high water mark" in your retirement plan account was probably the end of the 4th quarter of 1999.

In March of 2000, the stock market risk-management indicators began to suggest a higher level of risk in the stock market than most retirement plan investors would be willing to accept.

At that time, it would have been an appropriate risk-management strategy to make a couple of investment decisions in your retirement plan account. The first would have been to sell any mutual funds you owned at that time that had underperformed the overall stock market as measured by the S&P 500.

The reason to sell these underperforming mutual funds you owned would have been two-fold. One, if the mutual funds in question had not gone up as much as the overall stock market in a "good" stock market cycle, these same mutual funds would probably go down at a faster rate if the stock market cycle turned down. This concept is part of the Relative Strength tools I will talk about in Chapters Eight and Nine.

Second, as the stock market indicators suggest a higher-than-comfortable level of risk, a practical investment management move would be to take money that is currently invested in the stock market and go to the safety of the money market account in your retirement plan menu. "Take your profits" would be another way to explain the same investment management principle.

The concept in this second point is what failed most retirement plan investors in March of 2000. For many of these investors, the stock market "felt high" but they had no discipline or set of tools to help them come to the logical investment decision that would have allowed them to take some of their large gains out of the stock market and into the safety of the money market account.

Well, Portfolio A did not have access to the new stock market risk-management tools that you will learn to use and trust in the later chapters of this book. Portfolio A would be an example of the investment style that you might have used previously in the management of your retirement plan assets. Portfolio A is an example of doing nothing in the early stages of a stock market decline.

In March of 2000, the stock market begins to move lower, and Portfolio A rides the stock market through the down cycle fully exposed to the same mutual funds owned at the top of the stock market cycle.

Now, look at the investment results of Portfolio B. When the stock market risk-management indicators suggested a high risk level in March of 2000, Portfolio B raises cash in the four mutual fund positions it owned at that time.

REMAINING 100% INVESTED VERSUS RAISING SOME CASH

Situation A:
20% Market Decline

PORTFOLIO A:
RAISING NO CASH

	Intial Portfolio	After 20% Correction
Stock A	10,000	8,000
Stock B	10,000	8,000
Stock C	10,000	8,000
Stock D	10,000	8,000
Stock E	10,000	8,000
Stock F	10,000	8,000
Stock G	10,000	8,000
Stock H	10,000	8,000
Stock I	10,000	8,000
Stock J	10,000	8,000
	$100,000	**$80,000**

PORTFOLIO CHANGE: -20%
TO GET BACK TO EVEN: 25%

PORTFOLIO B:
RAISED 40% CASH

	Intial Portfolio	After 20% Correction
	10,000	8,000
	10,000	8,000
	10,000	8,000
	10,000	8,000
	10,000	8,000
	10,000	8,000
Cash	10,000	10,000
Cash	10,000	10,000
Cash	10,000	10,000
Cash	10,000	10,000
	$100,000	**$88,000**

PORTFOLIO CHANGE: -12%
TO GET BACK TO EVEN: 13.6%

There could have been a couple of reasons for this strategic investment move. Most likely the four mutual funds in Portfolio B were sold because they had not performed as well as the S&P 500 when the stock market had been rising prior to March 2000. The other reason for the sale of the four mutual funds would have been that these funds began to fall at a faster rate than the S&P 500 beginning in March 2000.

As a combination of the reasons listed above, the stock market exposure in Portfolio B was reduced from 100% to 60% beginning in March 2000. The final assumption in this example is that the stock market correction was 20% from the top to the bottom levels.

Portfolio B was down in value about 12%. Portfolio B had losses as well, but is in much better shape. As you see in the chart above, the mathematics of that example show that it takes a 13.6% increase in Portfolio B to get back to even. Portfolio A on the other hand has to increase 25% in value to get back to even.

A key point here is that Portfolio B had money in the retirement plan money market with the opportunity to reenter the stock market at the new lower price levels. Portfolio A did not.

This is a part of the example that is hard to quantify in investment return numbers. But common sense would tell you that if you have money to go back into the stock market once it stops falling and begins to go up, you will have better future investment returns than if you don't have a money market balance available. Is it easier to make money in the stock market if you have the money to invest when the stock market is "on sale"?

When the stock market indicators are suggesting high risk (these are the Bullish Percent concepts from Chapter Six), raising some cash in your retirement plan account is a way to hedge against potential stock market declines. When the indicators begin to stabilize and show signs of demand regaining control of the stock markets, you've got money to put back to work at lower risk levels. And the simple mathematics of the situation is that you don't need as much of an investment return to get back to even.

If the mutual fund positions you continue to hold in your retirement plan account are in strong Relative Strength (Chapters Eight and Nine), you are likely to see those mutual funds hold up better during a stock market decline. Strong Relative Strength mutual funds may not be down as much as the broad stock market averages which will also help the overall portfolio performance of your retirement plan account.

Just a reminder, below is the "get back to even" formula:

$$\frac{\textbf{Investment down by \%}}{\textbf{(100 minus \% down)}} = \frac{\textbf{\% return needed to}}{\textbf{get back to even}}$$

Portfolio A:
Investments down by 20%:

$$\frac{20}{(100-20)} = \frac{25\%}{80}$$

Portfolio B:
Investments down by 12%:

$$\frac{12}{(100-12)} = \frac{13.6\%}{88}$$

As you might expect, the same mathematics apply to an upward move in the stock market cycle. Again, Portfolio B would have the advantage here because of the money market balance is available to buy stocks back at lower price levels.

Situation B:
10% Market Rally

	Intial Portfolio	After 10% Rally		Intial Portfolio	After 10% Rally
Stock A	10,000	11,000		10,000	11,000
Stock B	10,000	11,000		10,000	11,000
Stock C	10,000	11,000		10,000	11,000
Stock D	10,000	11,000		10,000	11,000
Stock E	10,000	11,000		10,000	11,000
Stock F	10,000	11,000		10,000	11,000
Stock G	10,000	11,000	Cash 10,000	10,000
Stock H	10,000	11,000	Cash 10,000	10,000
Stock I	10,000	11,000	Cash 10,000	10,000
Stock J	10,000	11,000	Cash 10,000	10,000
	$100,000	**$110,000**		**$100,000**	**$106,000**

PORTFOLIO CHANGE: +10%   **PORTFOLIO CHANGE: +6%**

A CHANGE IN BEHAVIOR IS NEEDED

Buy-and-Hold is by far the most popular investment management policy for retirement plan investors, because it is the easiest to do. Set a course by investing in the mutual fund names you recognize in your retirement plan menu, and hope for the best.

Can you name one other area of your life where you have done the same thing the same way since you began your working career? Do you bank the same way you did when you received your first paycheck? Does your doctor rely on the same medical information that was available since you began your working career? Have your job skills stayed the same since you began working?

The answers to the above questions don't require a great deal of elaboration. If you manage your retirement plan today the same way you did when you began your working career, you have likely created unnecessary problems for yourself. The information provided in the later chapters of this book will give you the confidence you need to make changes in your current investment behavior.

Many of the current retirement plan advice tools have been exposed for what they are, and more importantly what they are not, in the last five years. These tools have forced the retirement plan participants into a buy-and-hold corner. And they have fewer and fewer years in which to fix their retirement plan management problems before it will be too late in the game.

To "stay the course" when the stock markets are performing badly is truly dangerous. To think that the mutual fund options available in your retirement plan are different, and that you are properly diversified, is just not correct. And to repeat the same thing in the future, when you are closer and closer to retirement, is simply foolish.

The money in your retirement plan has to be monitored and adjusted in light of changes in the economy, interest rates and stock market valuations. Just like the other areas in your life. The way you manage the money in your retirement plan has to change with the new realities of the stock and bond markets.

Historically, the problem has been that retirement plan investors did not have access to the professional tools and resources available to make better investment decisions with the money in their retirement plans. But that is not the case any more.

What I want to accomplish in this book, is to make retirement plan investors realize that the retirement plan advice environment has changed. With the Internet technology and resources available, any retirement plan participant can successfully manage his or her retirement plan menu using the same tools that were previously available only to investment professionals.

With the use of the right tools, or a relationship with an advisor who knows how to use the tools, any retirement plan participant can protect and grow the value of their retirement plan in any stock or bond market environment.

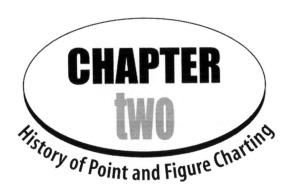

CHAPTER two

History of Point and Figure Charting

In the years that I have been providing risk-management advice to retirement plan participants, I have found out what works, and what does not. I have found out what retirement plan participants want, and what they don't. And most importantly, I know what retirement plan participants need in order to make better investment decisions on their retirement plan assets.

What retirement plan investors don't want is to be reminded of the investment concepts that they do not understand. These are the same investment concepts that they do not have the time--and in many cases the interest--to understand.

Since the top of the stock market cycle in March of 2000, retirement plan investors also are not in the mood for the unrestrained optimism that comes in a steady stream from the financial media.

Optimism is good in life because it keeps you healthy and resilient. But in the financial markets, optimism can hurt you in a big way.

Realism is the key. And you must have the ability to manage your retirement plan assets that reflect the current stock market *realities*.

The most pressing, basic question that a retirement plan participant has today is:

"Where do I invest the money in my retirement plan?"

You can tell that the answer to this question has nothing to do with what the stock market did last year, is doing this year or will do next year. The answer to this question has to do with where to be invested right now. Today.

Retirement plan investors want to feel like they are in control of the decisions they make in the management of their retirement plan accounts. They want to call their own shots in their retirement plans instead of guessing at what to own--and what to do next when the stock market begins to drop in value. Again.

Part of the control issue for retirement plan investors is the feeling that they don't want the value of their retirement plan returns tied directly to the roller coaster ride that has been the stock market of recent years. Many retirement plan investors I meet with feel a lack of control.

And I think a feeling of control takes the emotions out of the process of managing a retirement plan. Many investors are very frustrated about continually reacting emotionally to rising and falling stock markets. And they are tired of guessing at what to do next or what mutual fund option to buy now.

Control comes from confidence. And there is no confidence in retirement plan participants that I meet with that they are "doing the right thing" with their retirement plan money.

Managing one's retirement plan account just adds more to the pressures of life. It takes time away from family and career. And most of the retirement plan participants I meet with have no training about how to manage the risk with their large retirement plan account balances.

Retirement plan investors want easy-to-understand, customized and timely information on the menu of mutual fund options available to them in their retirement plans. They are not experts in this area of financial management, so they need information delivered from an honest and straightforward source that has their best interests in mind.

The reality of today is that most retirement plan participants don't get to their above-mentioned; they get financial media.

Every sound bite on television and article that fills the daily financial print, quotes "experts" who promote the upward movement of the stock market and the reasons for that direction.

The safest bet for the financial media to promote is that the stock market will go up. Both now, and over the long-term. The stock market always goes up over the long-term, right?

Think about it. Who is the biggest advertiser on both financial television and in financial print? That would be the mutual fund companies and the money management firms!

Who then, would be the biggest benefactor of the propagation of information that the stock market will always go up?

The last thing that retirement plan investors want is predictions or projections from computer-generated historical models. They want answers right now for their questions about what to own and what not to own--right now.

The vast majority of information that retirement plan providers pass off as "investment guidance," has none of the above data. There is not a printed brochure, Web site address, or retirement plan help desk employee that can answer any one of the above concerns that are most common to the retirement plan participants I work with.

So, part of the solutions that I will propose in this book will deal with the management of all the information that is available to retirement plan participants.

THIS IS NOT A NEW PROBLEM FOR STOCK MARKET INVESTORS.

I have tried to set the stage for the problems that confront retirement plan investors *today*. But, the person that said "we can learn a great deal from history" knew what he or she was talking about. History can serve as a valuable teacher when it comes to stock market investing.

Charles Dow, for example, had much of the same investment management issues back in the late 1800's that we have today. And he responded to them by developing the practice of charting stock price movements. That is, at the end of every day of stock market trading, Dow "figured" a picture of the price movement of the stocks he was interested in. These figures soon developed into charts.

The purpose of these charts was to present an accurate picture of the buying and selling action of each stock. These charts were totally unrelated to what self-interested stock market investors "told" the investing public to invest in. Charles Dow figured out that there were no disinterested parties in the stock market game. Just as Charles Dow would get calls and office visits from "tipsters," retirement plan investors today get radio, telephone, television, print, e-mail and Internet visits from the financial media with the same purpose. That is to help you make a decision for the "long-term" on what to do with the money in your retirement plan. Dow's stock charts were related only to what those interested parties in the stock market game were actually "doing" with their money.

Thus, the premise of Point & Figure charting is revealed. It is to provide a logical, organized and sensible way of recording the supply and demand relationship in any particular stock. The trends and inflection points on a stock chart will show clear levels of where buyers and sellers meet to determine the price of a stock.

If there are more buyers than there are sellers willing to sell, the price of that stock will rise. On the other hand, if there are more sellers than there are buyers willing to buy, then the price of that stock will decline. If buying and selling are equal, the price will remain the same. This is the irrefutable law of supply and demand. The same reasons that cause price fluctuations in tomatoes, gasoline or tickets to see your favorite local sports team cause price fluctuations in securities, too.

Charles Dow did not invent the economic forces of supply and demand, but he did help with the development of charts to show the relationship of those forces on the price of individual stocks.

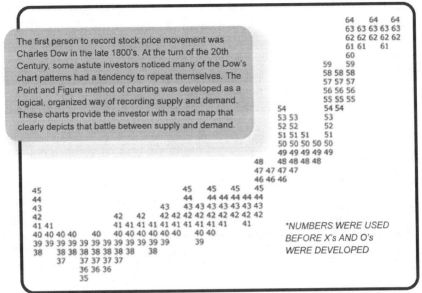

The first person to record stock price movement was Charles Dow in the late 1800's. At the turn of the 20th Century, some astute investors noticed many of the Dow's chart patterns had a tendency to repeat themselves. The Point and Figure method of charting was developed as a logical, organized way of recording supply and demand. These charts provide the investor with a road map that clearly depicts that battle between supply and demand.

*NUMBERS WERE USED
BEFORE X's AND O's
WERE DEVELOPED

Source: www.dorseywright.com

The chart above is courtesy of the Dorsey Wright Global Online University. It depicts the first style of Dow's Point & Figure charts where the price of the stock was recorded by price in columns which later were replaced by X's for ascending numbers and O's for descending numbers. In its simplest form, the chart pattern will indicate which force is winning the battle in an individual stock or stock market indicator--that is, supply or demand.

The financial media, at every opportunity, bombard investors with information on the merits and details of "what to buy." Entire industries have been built around the idea that one mutual fund is better to buy or own than another mutual fund.

But the Point & Figure Method of technical analysis is concerned only with the question of "when to buy" into the stock market as a whole or into an individual class or category of mutual fund. This part of the investment management process, and the critical question of "when to sell," is what is missing from the way most retirement plan participants make their retirement plan decisions.

Most retirement plan participants go about the investment management process completely backwards. They try to pick which mutual funds they should own in their retirement plan by beginning with the individual mutual fund. The better way to do this is to begin by determining if the stock market is on OFFENSE or DEFENSE, and what parts of the stock market offer the highest possible return for the lowest level of risk.

POINT & FIGURE BASICS

Again, the Point & Figure chart depicts the battle between supply and demand. There are two basic signals that develop. They are the Double Top Buy signal and the Double Bottom Sell signal. These are the two most basic patterns and everything else mentioned in this book will be based on these basic chart patterns.

A buy signal shows demand is in control of the stock or mutual fund price. It occurs when a column of X's exceeds the previous column of X's on the upside as show to the right:

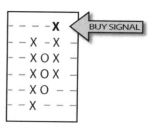

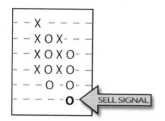

A sell signal shows supply is in control of the stock or mutual fund price. It occurs when a column of O's exceeds the previous column of O's on the downside as shown to the left.

The beauty of the Point & Figure Method of technical analysis is that there is no room for interpretation. A stock or mutual fund is either on a buy signal or a sell signal. Not both, only one at a time.

It makes no difference what the outlook for the stock market is, that interest rates or the U.S. dollar are rising or falling, or who won the last Super Bowl. If there are either more buyers than sellers in a stock or mutual fund, the price chart is in X's. If there are more sellers than buyers in a stock or mutual fund, the price chart is in O's.

Another more simple way to look at the "picture" of the supply versus demand relationship of a stock or mutual fund is to think of what the actual symbols on the price chart represent. Think in terms of this formula:

X's = WEALTH ACCUMULATION

O's = WEALTH PRESERVATION

At any time, when you look at the chart of a stock or mutual fund, you will know which economic force has taken control of that security. This information can be extremely useful in making the investment decision to buy or sell the stock or mutual fund.

You can take the time to keep up-to-date on the latest stock market forecasts, the next Federal Reserve meeting or the price target for gold. That is fine if you have the time to spend watching things that make no difference to how you should manage your retirement plan. Everything you ever need to know to make an informed decision on whether to buy, hold or sell a stock or a mutual fund full of stocks, can be found in the Point & Figure chart.

Charles Dow did not trust any financial information that was spoken or written in the 1800's, so why should we today? Why does anyone? There are no disinterested parties on Wall Street in regards to financial information.

The only thing that has changed from when Charles Dow first developed the use of Point & Figure charts in the late 1800's and today, is that there is MORE financial information available from MORE interested parties.

WHY POINT & FIGURE CHARTS ARE IMPORTANT

The massive amount of financial information available today—more precisely misinformation—requires that a retirement plan participant have some sort of filter as to what is important and relevant and what is not. A Point & Figure chart is as good of an investment tool for that filter as has been ever invented.

I always tell my retirement plan advice clients to remember that every time they look at a Point & Figure chart, they will get an honest answer to their most basic investment management questions:

- Should I be in the stock market right now?
- What is the risk of owning stocks at this time?
- Is the mutual fund I own in my retirement plan the best one available?

Large institutions control the price movement of the stock markets, the stocks and mutual funds that make up the stock markets, and the sectors and asset classes within the stock markets. That is the reality of the situation.

There is an old saying on Wall Street that, "The stock does not know you own it." That is just as true today in the management of stock market assets as it has ever been. No matter what the size of your retirement plan, it pales in comparison to the trillions of dollars that change hands every day in the world's stock markets.

When these large pools of investors decide to buy or sell, the Point & Figure chart will show you a "picture" of the movement of those dollars.

The Point & Figure chart does not have any relationship to what the experts "say" in the financial media. The Point & Figure chart only gives an unbiased picture of what these experts actually "do." The professionals on Wall Street vote with their money. And the professionals that manage the mutual fund options in your retirement plan menu vote with your money. The Point & Figure chart gives you the returns of that election. Every day.

CHAPTER
three
Your Retirement Plan Does Not Work

Since the inception of the 401(k) retirement plan in the early 1980's, there has been a standard, traditional approach in the communication pattern from the retirement plan sponsor/provider to the retirement plan participant. That is to provide only the most generic and hard-to-read statements as infrequently as the law allows.

To make your retirement plan offering easy to understand and efficient takes time and money. Most retirement plan sponsors are not going to spend either on the retirement plan offering.

On the other side of your retirement plan is the retirement plan provider. That provider contracts with your company for a certain level of services made available to retirement plan participants. No more and no less. The retirement plan provider gets paid on the number of participants in the retirement plan, and on the percentage of management fees based on the dollar value of the retirement plan. If that was how you were compensated, what would you be concerned about as the retirement plan provider?

The retirement plan statement is another area of neglect by the retirement plan sponsors and providers. I have simply never met one retirement plan participant who understands her quarterly retirement plan statement. And I know that I struggle with the copies of the retirement plan statements my clients provide me. And I have been viewing every generation of brokerage and retirement plan statements for the last two decades.

I have met with retirement plan participants in their offices, who have pulled out 15-20 unopened retirement plan quarterly statement envelopes from a bottom drawer in their credenza, and shown them to me. This stack of quarterly statements would represent four to five years of quarterly retirement plan statements--unseen by the participant.

Today, most retirement plan changes and updates come via e-mail. These e-mails do not get noticed, let alone read by retirement plan participants. There is an endless supply of brochures, manuals, newsletters and workshops thrown at retirement plan participants both in on-line and in-person formats. Many of these participants have commented to me that they could, if they wanted, make a second career out of selecting the tools available to them to manage their retirement plans.

But, the problem with these education materials is that the content is generic and provides information to the lowest common denominator of retirement plan participants. Information on "What is a mutual fund" is not going to be read by an even mildly sophisticated retirement plan participant.

Granted, the level of financial risk-management sophistication of a retirement plan participant is much lower than the myriad of retirement plan advice tools available. The example I like to use in my retirement plan advice practice is that of parking a Ferrari in the driveway of a fifteen-year-old's home that will soon get a learner's permit. The new driver has a great interest in driving any available automobile, but he or she does not have the experience necessary to enjoy driving a Ferrari. Similarly, most retirement plan investors begin to use the current generation of retirement planning tools, but they don't know how use them.

MAJOR CONFLICT OF INTERESTS

An advisory opinion issued by the Department of Labor in December 2001 allowed the mutual fund companies to provide investment advice to retirement plan participants, provided that they contract with an outside supplier for that advice.

24

Soon after this ruling, alliances were created between the major retirement plan custodians and providers—Fidelity, Merrill Lynch, Vanguard, etc.—and the major mutual fund and asset allocation data providers—Financial Engines, Ibbotson and Morningstar.

How independent can this investment advice product be, when the advice provider is being paid by the retirement plan administrator? Is Morningstar going to recommend that a retirement plan sponsor kick several high-cost Fidelity mutual funds out of the retirement plan menu if the retirement plan provider is Fidelity Retirement Plan Services Company? I don't think so.

I think the cozy relationship between the retirement plan providers and the third-party "independent" advice providers is another example of what a great job the financial services industry has done in brainwashing the American investing public into thinking that the days of outperforming the broad stock market averages are over.

Today U.S. stock market investors in general—and that includes retirement plan participants—don't expect or look for great stock market strategies. The stock market investors of today only are being offered sophisticated computer programs that present cookie-cutter strategic asset allocation models.

The entire U.S. financial services advisors have become so afraid of litigation, that they no longer provide active, professional stock market risk management. Instead, these financial professionals only know to tell their stock market clients to allocate among several asset classes and rebalance their stock market accounts twice a year.

NOT FOR THE PLAN PARTICIPANT'S BENEFIT

When on-line retirement plan advice tools were first introduced a few years ago, they were heralded as the future of the retirement plan industry. No, you have not missed anything because that has not happened.

Petrified of potential employee retirement plan participant lawsuits, corporations (retirement plan sponsors) began relying several years ago on 401(k) advice from firms such as Financial Engines, Morningstar and Ibbotson.

The thought here was that canned investment risk questionnaires buried in lively PowerPoint presentations and delivered via company retirement plan Web sites would succeed where over twenty years of retirement plan education materials failed.

I have met with many retirement plan participants that do not know the Web site address, log-in procedure, or account ID and password to their retirement plan provider. The current generation of on-line, print and e-mail communications from both retirement plan sponsors and providers has consistently left retirement plan participants exposed to both the top and bottom of recent stock market trends, substantial losses, and high annual retirement plan costs.

There are no on-line retirement plan tools available that can answer the most basic questions that retirement plan participants have. That is, "Am I doing the right thing with my retirement plan money? Where do I invest my money now? What do I do if the stock market changes?"

Investment professionals organize their days, even their careers, around the logical and disciplined process necessary to sort through the mountains of available investment news, information and analysis. For the non-investment industry retirement plan participant, that just is not possible in this day and age.

So the normal, every day, working-to-get-ahead retirement plan participant puts off even the most basic asset allocation and mutual fund selection decisions because they are too painful to make. These retirement plan investors think they can't make the intelligent decisions that are necessary in order to manage their retirement plans the right way, so they do nothing at all.

WHAT RETIREMENT PLAN PARTICIPANTS DON'T GET FOR THEIR FEES

The first question that comes to mind is, "Why are we paying the managers of the mutual funds, when we have to do our own investment management activity?" As a retirement plan participant, you are already paying fees and trading costs of 1.5% to 2.0% annually to the mutual funds you own in your retirement plan.

If you look at it from another angle, you are already paying these mutual fund companies a sizable annual amount to "manage" your retirement plan balances. If you add another layer of costs on top of the existing ones, at what point does it get to be a ridiculous cost for the amount of return on investment?

It is not enough to pay the mutual fund companies you choose to manage the money in your retirement plan. In addition, you have to pay to have tools available that take the stock market investment process out of the hands of the mutual fund manager, and put it back into yours? Do you have time for that? Or the knowledge and experience?

What are these mutual fund managers doing for the fees they are already receiving? Shouldn't an "allocation" out of a clearly declining stock market environment be one of the investment management functions of the mutual fund manager?

Or how about taking a little bit of the mutual fund that you have hired him or her to manage, and "rebalance" some of that mutual fund into a stock that is performing better than the overall stock market? Instead, you've likely been riding that stock both up and down during the most recent stock market cycles.

The question becomes for a retirement plan participant, "What investment management skill and acumen are the money managers (that manage the mutual fund options in my company retirement plan) actually providing for their annual management fees and trading costs?" The answer to that question lies in the growth of your retirement plan value in the last few years.

If you try this calculation at home, remember to reduce the current value of your retirement plan account by the amount of your contributions and your employer-matching retirement plan contributions. Do so for each year. And then figure out what the real return on your money invested in those previous years was.

Do you see where the on-line retirement planning tools are just another layer of fees for the retirement plan provider? And they provide a layer of fiduciary protection for the retirement plan sponsor.

I think it gets down to the way the information is presented to the retirement plan participant. As you know, for years and years the retirement plan sponsor was in the background, never wanting to give the retirement plan participant the impression that they, in any way, would recommend one retirement plan option over another option.

Now, with the help of the retirement plan provider, your retirement plan sponsor's biggest problem is to communicate--in new ways--to you all the latest and greatest features that are include in your retirement plan.

Now you have it all: retirement plan calculators, performance reports, pie charts, Morningstar® reports, online statements, investment education, retirement planning tools, etc. It is almost as if your retirement plan sponsor, with the help of the retirement plan provider, can't help you enough.

DO YOU SMELL THE SAME THING I DO?

I don't know how any rational person could look at this situation in any other way. I know I can't. I have sliced and diced the numbers every way I know how. I have read hundreds and hundreds of retirement plan industry articles written by both professionals inside and outside of the retirement plan business.

Most importantly, I have seen with my own eyes, the real performance numbers from real-life retirement plan investors. I am sure these people are the same type of retirement plan investors that are reading this information right now. The numbers don't lie. And the lack of performance, or any real growth, does not lie either.

IT IS TWO-AGAINST-ONE. AND YOU ARE THE ONE.

I hope the discussion of these important retirement plan realities make retirement plan participants think in a different way about what is actually going on in their retirement plans.

I don't mean to promote a battle between retirement plan participants and retirement plan sponsors and their partners, retirement plan providers. But what is, is. That is the way the retirement plan world works. You can analyze and examine the information from any side that you want, and the results will be the same.

For the retirement plan sponsor, the company retirement plan is a "cost of doing business." There is no way that most companies can attract and keep good employees without a retirement plan in place. Most importantly, companies are very cost-conscious today. (Insert your own cheap company story here).

The only way a retirement plan sponsor is going to add another layer of fees or costs involved in a retirement plan offering, is if those costs are going to benefit more than just the retirement plan participants. Those costs of the current generation of retirement plan tools are more for the benefit, and fiduciary insulation, of the company.

For the retirement plan provider, it is a numbers game on two fronts. The first front is that the more money there is in the company retirement plan, the more investment management fees are generated. And the retirement plan participants are the ones with the money in the retirement plan.

The second front is that the retirement plan provider will provide only the level of service that is contracted with the retirement plan sponsor. That means more and more automation of the retirement plan offering. And it means more and more tools become available that a retirement plan participant either does not know exist, or does not have the time or expertise to figure out how to use.

The retirement plan sponsor and the retirement plan provider are the Two in this equation. The retirement plan participant is the One.

CHAPTER four

The Latest Industry Trends Will Not Work

In this chapter I want to continue the discussion of the problems with the latest and greatest retirement plan bells and whistles that have been offered to retirement plan participants in the recent years. I want to explain the shortcomings of each of these retirement plan offerings in more detail.

The three most recent retirement plan offerings have been personal retirement plan advice, life cycle mutual funds, and computer-generated Monte Carlo simulation models.

If you did not realize that any or all of the three options were available to you in your retirement plan, don't worry. Sometimes when you are too busy to pay attention, and follow the crowd of other retirement plan investors that are desperate for any help they can get in the management of their retirement plans, you do the right thing by default. The right thing here is to stay away from each of these three offerings in your retirement plan.

PERSONAL ADVICE FOR RETIREMENT PLAN PARTICIPANTS

It is going to sound strange that I am going to "beat up" the offering of personal retirement plan advice, in a book that advocates the very same concept. My only answer is that there are good reasons that you are offered investment advice in your retirement plan, and there are bad reasons.

In addition, there is a big difference between good investment advice and bad investment advice. Just like there is a big difference between investment advice that will harm you, and investment advice that will hurt you.

Since the Department of Labor ruling 96-1 in December of 2001, more and more large retirement plan sponsors have made on-line personal financial advice available for employees that participate in the company retirement plan.

At face value, you would think that is a good thing. You'd think that someone has learned some very valuable lessons from the brutal bear market beating that retirement plan investors have taken in recent years. However, like many things in the business world today, the reality is much different than the reason behind the reality.

The driving force for company retirement plan sponsors in making any level of retirement plan advice available to retirement plan participants is a re-emergence of the retirement plan sponsor as a fiduciary who is liable as a retirement plan trustee.

The reality of the offering is not that the company retirement plan sponsors all of a sudden adopted a more benevolent and compassionate attitude towards their current employees and retirement plan participants. The reality is that company retirement plan trustees do not want to be sued by the current generation of retirement plan participants when upon retirement they have no where near the money they need to live another thirty years.

The same thing can be said for the major retirement plan administrators—Fidelity, Vanguard, T. Rowe Price—offering managed account services to retirement plan participants. As I talked about in the last chapter, the door was opened to offering these investment management services to retirement plan participants by the Department of Labor ruling in December 2001.

These retirement account management services are provided by third-party database firms like Financial Engines, Morningstar, and Ibbotson. These services include asset allocation and periodic account rebalancing.

INDUSTRY CREDENTIALS PROVIDE INSIDE INFORMATION

I have not mentioned previously in this book, that I am an Accredited Investment Fiduciary (AIF™). This designation is granted by the Center for Fiduciary Studies, an organization that was established as a full-time training and research facility focused exclusively on investment fiduciary responsibility and portfolio management.

Many retirement plan investor clients are surprised to learn that, as an SEC-registered RIA, I become a co-fiduciary on their retirement plan assets in my role as an advisor to them. Both my firm and I have a fiduciary responsibility in the investment advice we provide to a retirement plan participant.

I thought it would be a good idea for my professional development to pursue this designation when it was first offered. The training and information I receive has not helped me at all on the investment management side of my business. But I have a much deeper understanding of the responsibilities involved in providing retirement plan advice to my clients. And that helps give my clients more peace of mind.

As with any professional designation, there are annual education requirements that must be met to maintain the designation. Yearly, I either attend a meeting or sit-in on conference calls in order to secure enough continuing education hours to keep my designation.

The reason I mention this information is because of the content I am privy to in these meetings and conference calls. And the hottest topic is what steps retirement plan sponsors can take now to insulate themselves, in their roles as retirement plan fiduciaries, from any retirement plan participant lawsuits in the future.

Every major retirement plan provider is offering fiduciary liability education and compliance with the Department of Labor and ERISA laws in their current marketing documents.

On more than one occasion in these education forums, the speaker is an ERISA lawyer. It is common knowledge within the legal community that retirement plan providers are in the crosshairs of the litigators in the near future. ERISA lawyers spend a great deal of their time providing information to the litigation attorneys about the current breaches in fiduciary liability by retirement plan sponsors.

It makes sense if you think about it. If you are thinking about lawsuits in the future filed by retirement plan participants who will claim that they were never given the sufficient tools and information necessary to both build and maintain adequate retirement plan balances in order to prepare them for a secure retirement you have to have a good grasp of the facts about the retirement plan offering during your working career.

These litigation attorneys cannot rely on the memory of their clients as to the facts and circumstances regarding their participation in the company retirement plan. So they are building their future case files now while the facts and circumstances are available.

Making the tools and resources available to retirement plan participants is the only thing that is required of a retirement plan sponsor. If these tools are generic, unspecific and based on historical data, that is not the fault of the retirement plan sponsor because current ERISA law does not require any more. The current availability of the resources is more important, in the long run to the retirement plan sponsor, than if these tools actually do the job they are supposed to do----which in theory, is to help the retirement plan participants better manage their retirement plan accounts.

IT IS A PROBLEM WITH SOCIETY

The problem is not just with retirement plan sponsors. Think now about all of the recent examples you have heard and read about in your daily life that convince you that in our society today, no one wants to take responsibility for their own actions.

Start with the lady who spilled hot coffee on her lap in the McDonald's drive-thru and got all those millions of dollars a few years ago. And don't forget those thousands of retirement plan participants at Enron and WorldCom that lost all of their retirement plan money because it was invested in their company stock. Those cases have almost everything to do with the focus on retirement plan sponsor liability in the retirement plan industry now.

Fast-forward to the day you retire or maybe a few months or a year after that. By that time you have had a chance to figure out, along with your spouse, that all this money you have saved in your retirement plan is not as much as you thought it was. And the money "does not go as far as it did in the old days." I am sure you heard that phrase at one time or another from your parents.

So what do you do then? You sue your previous employer because you don't have enough money to retire. The grounds of the lawsuit would be that your former employer, (the company retirement plan sponsor), and the retirement plan provider, did not provide you the right amount of investment options, tools, education, resources, etc.

The same day that you are reading this book, there are teams of litigators documenting every single piece of retirement plan information and offering. The retirement plan sponsor, through the help of the retirement plan provider, will have document after document, e-mail after e-mail, brochure after brochure, and conference room meeting announcement after conference room meeting announcement regarding all of the retirement plan investment tools you had available to you during your years of employment at your company.

The recent volatile stock market environment has placed a spotlight on this fiduciary liability squarely on the shoulders of the retirement plan sponsor. Remember how the system works: the retirement plan sponsor is the client of the retirement plan provider, so the provider will provide whatever goods and services that are necessary to keep the retirement plan sponsor happy and out of the court room.

LIFESTYLE AND LIFECYCLE ASSET ALLOCATION FUNDS

By far, the most popular new offering in the core menu of retirement plan mutual funds in recent years has been the "lifestyle" and "lifecycle" asset allocation mutual funds. These funds offer premixed stock and bond market portfolios through a single mutual fund option in a retirement plan menu.

Lifestyle mutual funds typically refer to mutual funds that allocate the fund's assets to predetermined models—like Conservative, Balanced or Moderate investment models. The retirement plan participant selects a third-party money manager that selects and monitors the participant's account, and rebalances the account every quarter. This form of lifestyle mutual funds would be built around a specific asset allocation model.

Lifecycle mutual funds typically refer to specific targeted retirement dates, like 2010, 2015 or 2020. In this type of mutual fund, the retirement plan participant selects the specific fund that best fits his or her retirement date, then that fund manager automatically rebalances the mutual fund assets every quarter. This form of lifestyle mutual fund would be built around specific retirement dates. These mutual funds are invested to automatically grow more conservative—less ownership of stocks—as they approach a targeted retirement date.

In both these types of mutual funds, the retirement plan participant delegates both the selection of individual mutual fund or funds, and the asset allocation decisions, to the mutual fund manager. The sales pitch on these investment options in a retirement plan menu is that you can "set-it-and-forget-it" and buy-and-hold your way to a secure retirement.

Many of these models are "passive" in nature. Once the target asset allocations are determined, they are rarely changed. For example, if you are currently 45 years-old, and would like to retire when you are 60-years-old, you would be a candidate to place the bulk of your retirement plan assets in a lifestyle mutual fund that had the number 2020 in its name. That number in the mutual fund name would correspond to the year in which you would retire.

In concept, retirement plan management and investing does not get any easier than choosing an asset allocation lifestyle mutual fund. The basic concept is enticing—invest in a fund with a predetermined asset allocation based on your desired risk tolerance or expected retirement date, sit back, and let the fund managers make the appropriate allocation decisions for you. No fuss, no muss.

If you currently see these pre-packaged asset allocation mutual funds offered in your retirement plan menu, you will surely recognize the names of the mutual fund companies that offer these products. At the end of 2004, fifty-five fund companies offered lifecycle mutual fund products, including such heavyweights as Fidelity Investments, The Vanguard Group and T. Rowe Price.

In your on-line retirement plan research and marketing material, these lifestyle mutual funds can go by any number of financial industry buzzwords---lifecycle, lifestyle, target-date, target-risk, target-retirement and target-allocation funds. If you see any of these names on your on-line retirement plan menu of options, now you know what they mean.

According to conventional wisdom, a 25-year-old person should invest in an aggressive portfolio that's top-heavy in equities. Because target-risk funds essentially maintain the same allocation mix over time, that same investor should rotate into a less-aggressive fund when he reaches middle age. Older investors, or the very risk-averse, should stick with conservative allocation mixes with greater exposure to bonds.

In summary, the further out the date on the lifestyle fund, the greater the exposure to the stock market. The closer you are to retirement, the greater the exposure to bonds and bond mutual funds. These funds automatically rebalance their portfolios toward more conservative allocations as they go through time and draw closer to their specified retirement year.

Now for some tough questions. Why would it be logical to offer a retirement plan investor a pre-packaged product that would give the illusion of a "set-it-and-forget-it" approach to managing retirement plan assets? Where in the history of stock market investment returns has that type of investment management approach been possible?

I think that faced with the real possibility of fiduciary breaches by the retirement plan sponsors, these lifestyle mutual funds are thought to be more ammunition for the retirement plan providers to avoid fiduciary liability. The hope is that these new "commoditized" retirement plan options will help the retirement plan provider avoid the continuation of the horror stories about self-directed retirement plan investors butchering their retirement portfolios through lack of knowledge and poor decisions.

The potential to avoid stock market losses by investing in a pre-packaged product that "automatically rebalances" is not logically possible. But I really don't think the retirement plan providers, and their clients--the retirement plan sponsors, realize or care about logic.

For the retirement plan provider, it is all about price. With the new popularity of the lifestyle mutual funds, retirement plan providers have turned retirement plan menus into the same style of offerings that you see on the menu at McDonald's.

At McDonald's, the menu is all about packages and making one decision on one package. You have to work harder to just order a single menu item like a hamburger. Most customers order a pre-packaged meal like a Happy Meal or McChicken Meal.

I have found the same problem in working with the new pre-packaged Lifestyle mutual funds now available in most large retirement plan menus. The retirement plan sponsor thinking seems to be that it must be easier for a retirement plan participant to make one investment decision, than four or five decisions. But what if the package is a bad decision?

LIFECYCLE FUND.....PIE CHART......SAME DIFFERENCE

Both a Lifecycle mutual fund and the pie chart asset allocation theory that it is based on, are in effect, a zero sum game. If you make an investment decision to allocate your retirement plan assets into a specific Lifecycle mutual fund, you then have fewer assets available to invest in any other asset class.

To further compound the investment decision problem, you also have to choose what Lifecycle fund to own, and what percentage of your retirement plan account to invest in that mutual fund option.

All Lifecycle mutual funds recommend a large part of your stock market exposure to be allocated in Large Cap stocks. As we have talked about previously, the S&P 500 or something close to that mix is the vehicle most often made available in the retirement plan menu.

Below is a moderately aggressive asset allocation model. This type of asset allocation model can be found in several places on the Internet and in the available on-line retirement plan toolbox of several retirement plan provider Web sites.

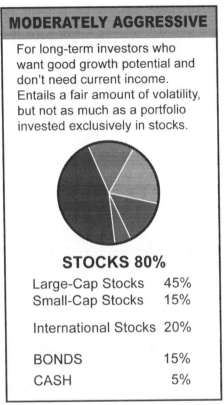

MODERATELY AGGRESSIVE

For long-term investors who want good growth potential and don't need current income. Entails a fair amount of volatility, but not as much as a portfolio invested exclusively in stocks.

STOCKS 80%

Large-Cap Stocks	45%
Small-Cap Stocks	15%
International Stocks	20%
BONDS	15%
CASH	5%

Source: Schwab.com

This picture can be applied to both a Life cycle mutual fund portfolio as well as an asset allocation strategy. Remember that both of these financial industry products are pre-packaged in order to cut down on the number of decisions required to manage financial assets.

As you see, the Moderately Aggressive model is suitable for an investment profile "for long-term investors who want good growth potential and don't need current income." In my experience, that would include the vast majority of current retirement plan investors.

The only problem is that putting 45% of your current retirement plan assets into Large Cap Stocks and 15% into bonds has not been a profitable strategy for over five years. That is the same asset allocation strategy that lost massive amounts of your retirement plan value beginning in March 2000.

As you now know, Small Cap Stocks have outperformed Large Cap Stocks, Bonds and Money Market over the last five years. Then why invest 65% of your available retirement plan account in the asset classes that are performing the worst over the last five years?

For this packaged service, Lifestyle mutual funds can charge an additional fee for management and other expenses in addition to the normal level of mutual fund management fees. Who gains those fees? The retirement plan sponsor (your company) shares in those increased management fees.

We have already discussed the lack of real investment management that mutual fund managers bring to the table to retirement plan investors. These lifestyle mutual funds make me all the more suspicious accordingly.

These new lifestyle mutual fund offerings have been "sold" to retirement plan sponsors under the guise of "fiduciary liability." Am I the only investment professional that sees this happening?

At what point does the menu of options available to a retirement plan participant have more to do with how the money is actually managed, and less to do about the retirement plan provider "selling the latest gadget" to the retirement plan sponsor?

On the stock market investment management side of this issue, let me ask a few common sense questions. These questions would be directed to a 55-year-old retirement plan investor who has been advised to buy the lifestyle fund with the 2010 number in it with his or her retirement plan assets. That would be thought to be a suitable investment based on this person's retirement age.

1. In May of 2005, are we at a cyclically high point in interest rates or a cyclically low point in interest rates in the history of the United States?

2. In the next five years, do you think the next dramatic movement in interest rates is going to be lower or higher?

3. Has anyone involved in the offering of this type of lifestyle mutual fund taken the time to inform the retirement plan participant of the relationship between interest rates and bond prices?

Then why would a retirement plan investor nearing retirement invest 75 to 85 percent of his or her retirement plan assets into a mutual fund that will take a dramatic drop in value when, not if, interest rates begin to rise?

40

I hope I made my point clear to you. As I will try to throughout this book, I have tried to use real-life examples to expose the fallacy of what I see passing for professional investment advice in retirement plans.

I would make the same argument on the stock market investment management side of lifestyle mutual funds. Does a 25-year-old retirement plan investor care less about losing large chunks of money in his or her retirement plan than a 55-year-old retirement plan investor?

In my experience, each of these retirement plan investors cares equally about losing money in their retirement plans. The only difference is that a 25-year-old retirement plan investor has more time to make the losses back. That would be the past losses from stocks, not the future losses from bond funds. A 55-year-old does not have that kind of time.

MONTE CARLO SIMULATION TOOLS

The lack of available time and useable investment management tools to make retirement plan decisions more successful are tough enough on retirement plan participants. Now retirement plan investors are being urged to use statistics and probability to help them make better investment management decisions in their retirement plans.

Monte Carlo simulation is a sophisticated and complex tool in which a computer simulates thousands upon thousands of potential investment outcomes. The calculations are based on varied data and assumptions, including an investor's asset allocation, years to and/or in retirement and the amount being periodically saved and withdrawn.

The Monte Carlo calculator is meant to simulate every possible outcome that could happen to a stock market portfolio. By using today's computing power to run thousands of calculations instead of one fixed-rate possibility, stock market investors can now obtain an entire range of answers.

After the computer gets done crunching the numbers, investors learn what percent chance they have of reaching their goals. The range of possibilities is from 0% to 100%. Any outcome above 70% and the stock market investor can feel fairly confident of meeting his or her retirement investing goals. Any outcome less than that, and the financial professional user has to go back and readjust the input data.

Let me stop right here. Does that description of the tool make any sense to you in helping manage your retirement plan assets? Would knowing the percent chance you have in retiring when you want to help you make better investment decisions, right now, in your retirement plan?

I could stop right here with the foolishness of this tool as a helpful investment decision-maker. But I have to go on...There is more to this madness.

Other on-line retirement plan tools use the far simpler concept of taking average annual returns of various investments and again using computers to come up with the correlation of historical returns to current asset allocation. If there's a shortfall in your progression towards your retirement goal, these tools simply tell the retirement plan investor to save more, change the asset allocation or change the year of retirement.

This type of retirement plan tool goes back to my example in Chapter One about the annual return assumptions of 10-12%. This tool really does use the concept that, "stocks are volatile year-to-year, but over the long term you get 10 percent." The theory here is to buy-and-hold and rebalance periodically, and you will be fine in retirement.

Monte Carlo simulation is far more technical than other on-line retirement planning tools. The Monte Carlo concept was developed during World War II by mathematicians seeking ways to understand the behavior of neutrons. It must have worked because we won World War II. But today it is being marketed to retirement plan participants to help them understand behavior of a different sort -- the markets and themselves.

The Monte Carlo tool is supposed to give retirement plan investors a realistic picture of what could happen as they approach their retirement age. In addition, the Monte Carlo tool is supposed to make the concept of "risk" easier for retirement plan investors to understand.

Again, I just have to stop early into this explanation. What do the behaviors of neutrons have to do with the behavior of stock market mutual funds?

In mid-year 2005, Wachovia retirement plan Web site announced the introduction of new retirement planning tools available to Wachovia clients through Wachovia financial advisers, "Monte Carlo is good for giving you a better, not perfect, sense of the uncertainty of meeting investment goals."

The main problem with Monte Carlo simulations is that they require the use of reasonable assumptions, projected investment returns and rates of inflation. So, in other words, if you put "garbage in," the investor will get "garbage out." If you use one wrong assumption about future stock market returns or the future rate of inflation, you will not get even close to a useful answer.

It is common knowledge among even the most sophisticated and experienced Monte Carlo simulation users that the tool is intended to produce a 70% chance of success of reaching your retirement investment goals. So that means that you have to be comfortable with at least a 30% chance of not being able to retire when and how you want to!

How is it possible that in the most economically powerful country in the world, that retirement plan tools like Monte Carlo are even considered legitimate? How is it tolerated by retirement plan participants that this tool could even remotely be helpful in making better investment decisions in their retirement plans?

Instead of worrying, or trying to project what the stock markets are going to give you for investment returns in the future, why not develop some risk-management tools that would allow retirement plan investors to make better investment decisions now? How many other industries worry 100% of the time about the future, and make no decisions on what to do with the changing business environments today?

Let's say you are 45 years old. If I asked you to name the next four people to be named President of the United States, what would be your success rate? And would your answer have one thing to do with how you would manage your retirement plan assets over the next fifteen years of your working career?

Isn't that the same thing that Monte Carlo is trying to do? With no thought at all to the changing economic, social and business circumstances over the next fifteen years, this tool is going to help you with your retirement plan investment management by giving you a percent chance of success? Fifteen years from now?

If a Monte Carlo simulation was a useful tool in the business world, it would have been successfully used in the management of stock market investments since most readers of this book have been alive. It has not been found to be useful. And it is not a useful stock market investment management tool just because it can be found on your retirement plan Web site.

There is an old business adage that states, "Some products are bought, and some products are sold." Monte Carlo simulations were "sold" by retirement plan providers, and were "bought" by retirement plan sponsors. And retirement plan participants were not given a useful stock market investment management tool in the process.

CHAPTER
five

Forget the Pie... Have Your Cake and Eat It Too

In the July/August 1986 issue of *Financial Analyst Journal,* the team of Brinson, Hood and Beebower published an article entitled, "Determinants of Portfolio Performance." The financial planning and investment management business was changed forever by the way the financial services industry interpreted this information.

Since that time, stock and bond market investors have been told that asset allocation among stocks, bonds and cash is the most important investment decision to make. The decision to allocate your investments among those three asset classes determines more than 93% of your investment return according to the above study.

The entire growth of financial planning and the "management" of your stock and bond market investments during the late 1980's and entire 1990's was based on conclusions of the above study. The financial service firms through the financial media have time and time again sold this concept to individual stock market and retirement plan investors.

I think that the reason the concept of pie chart asset allocation has grown to be part of every single retirement plan investment management resource offering is very simple. Who doesn't like pictures? Especially color pictures? The pictures make it easy to understand where to buy-and-hold your retirement plan assets.

To have the ability to go on-line and pull up the nice picture of where your retirement plan assets are currently invested, and where they should be invested, is about as easy as it gets. And Americans want easy. Even with their retirement plan assets.

The concept of the pie charts is a great one. The fact that some very well respected investment managers and financial academics have done studies that validate this information make the pie chart concept of asset allocation a good place to start for any retirement plan participant.

As you already know, when you log-on to your current retirement plan provider Web site, you will find a screen that summarizes your current retirement plan allocation among both asset classes and individual mutual fund options. Unfortunately, that is as far as most retirement plan participants get in the asset allocation process.

THIS IS WHERE THE PIE GETS BAD

There is a perception that investment management comes with the pie chart asset allocation tools available in your retirement plan. This notion can be hazardous to your retirement health. Retirement plan participants think that they will receive the answers they look for in the management of their retirement plan assets by viewing and automatically updating their pie charts. That concept is not correct.

The pie chart concept of managing stock and bond market risk in a retirement plan menu of options is an illusion. There has never been a case where a computer-generated pie chart has increased investment performance or reduced stock market risk in a retirement plan account. It has never happened.

I am not saying that asset allocation in the form of a pie chart does not work. The theory is a good place to start. My goal for the remainder of this book is to give you the tools necessary to make more informed decisions, with confidence, based on what your retirement plan asset pie chart tells you.

The second part of the pie chart illusion is that the assets will be rebalanced over time and the percentage of each asset class owned will be "automatically" stable. This rebalancing is also a product of the computer model which uses performance history as a guide.

One personal business observation here, if I may, in order to destroy this automatic rebalancing devil:

I have provided retirement plan advice to individual retirement plan participants for years. Not one time have I ever told one of my clients to sell a mutual fund that was going up at a faster rate than the overall stock markets. Then, suggest that right away, take the money from that sale and invest it in one of their retirement plan mutual fund options that was lagging the stock market performance at that time. In fact, I tell my clients that if I ever come up with a screw-ball investment strategy like that for them, they should fire me immediately.

Why would you sell what is working in your retirement plan, and buy more of what is not working in your retirement plan? Just because a computer told you to do it? Based on your age and retirement date? That is the entire concept of rebalancing.

In my retirement plan advisory practice, I can't blame poor investment performance on what information a computer gave me. My clients don't accept that. And I tell my clients to fire me if I ever come up with that as an explanation, too.

My clients pay me for the retirement plan advice I provide them. And part of that advice is to not make the same mistakes that most retirement plan investors make. The retirement plan advice I provide cannot afford to be stuck in one place at all times, and then only called to action once per year on an anniversary date. My advice has to work better than that.

THE PIE CHART CAN BE FIXED, BUT YOU CAN'T

The problem with the pie chart concept of managing a retirement plan account is that it is a fixed concept. The thought is that if you stick to your asset allocation model, that process will allow your retirement plan investment returns to be stable in the future.

There is a lot more here that goes into the asset allocation concept. But I don't want to get into the concepts of extrapolating historical stock and bond market returns, risk premiums, standard deviations and asset class correlations.

My intention when I set out to write this book was to inform you of the tools currently available to make better stock market risk-management decisions in your retirement plan. I don't want to give you theories. I want to inform you about the facts.

The pie chart concept is based on statistical extrapolations based on the historical returns of asset classes. How does that help you, today, to know what mutual funds to pick in your retirement plan menu? And how does that help you when the stock market risk changes in the future?

Every pie chart asset allocation model you will ever be exposed to will keep you more fully invested in the Large Cap mutual fund options available in your retirement plan menu. That is just the way it is, mainly because of the historical performance of owning Large Cap stocks.

If you are an aggressive investor in your retirement plan provider Investor Profile, you would be allocated towards 50% Large Cap stocks, 20% Small Cap stocks and the remaining 30% in International stocks. This investment approach works very well when the stock markets are configured to make money, and the rising tide of the stock markets allows all stocks to rise in value.

But what happens if Large Cap stocks stop going up at a faster rate than Small or Mid Cap stocks? Or what happens if Value stocks go up at a faster rate than Growth stocks? Those two questions describe the stock market environment we have lived through since the middle of 2000 until the beginning of 2005.

On February 17, 2000 the S&P 600 Small Cap Index began to "outperform" the S&P 500 Index. I will explain more on the investment management tools and concept used to determine this information in Chapters Eight and Nine. For now, just focus on the fact that you will soon be able to have access to the performance-based concept of Relative Strength. Relative Strength concepts are essential and powerful. You will be able to know at *any* time, whether you should be invested in Small or Mid Cap stocks, or Large Cap stocks.

More importantly, the information that is available will be provided on a real-time basis. The information has not one thing to do with historical returns, your current and future retirement ages, or "how much risk you want to take." The "outperformance" information is unbiased and unfiltered, and it answers the question of "What do I own in my retirement plan right now?"

In the period from February 17, 2000 to March 31, 2005, the S&P 600 Small Cap Index went up in value about 53.1%. During the same period the S&P 500 Index went down in value about 15.0%. That is a performance gap of 68.1%

Let me provide another example, over a similar time frame, for the other great question that you need to have answered in the management of your retirement plan assets. That is, "Do I own Value stocks or Growth stocks now?"

In the period from October 10, 2000 to March 31, 2005, the S&P BARRA Value Index fell in value about .91%. During the same period the S&P BARRA Growth Index fell in value about 28.1%.

No matter what the computer said about historical returns and the pie chart asset allocation model that guided your overexposure to Large Cap Growth stocks. The computer was wrong! The computer was wrong enough over that five year period to do some serious principal damage in your retirement plan account.

HOW TO FIX THE PIE

Let me interject a little common sense here. The computer models you use in your day-to-day business management are the same ones that spit out the asset allocation pie chart information that is supposed to help you manage your retirement plan assets. How accurate would your business models be if they made no changes over a five-year period?

Let me ask this equally unintelligent question. How long would any business continue to be a success if every quarter, it took money, time and resources away from the part of the business that was providing the best return on the investment, and reallocated the company money, time and resources to the part of the business that might begin to improve?

I want to make sure you read my question in the right way. I am asking you about the logic involved in getting rid of what works and making a bigger investment in what is not working, all because a computer provided you with the information. You may be historically right in your decision some time in the future, but it's a gamble.

I urge you to begin managing your retirement plan assets like you currently help your company manage its business. That is, by having a basic business strategy that is formed in part by historical facts, but makes the necessary management changes as the realities of the current business environment dictate.

Learn how to make your retirement plan investment decisions based on the reality of the current stock market environment. You can't change "what is," so learn how to make the investment management decisions in your retirement plan based on that fact.

How successful would you be if you drove home from work tonight looking in your rear view mirror, instead of looking through your windshield? The answer I am looking for is "not very successful."

It is the same thing with the pie chart asset allocation model. Investment returns cannot be anticipated because the stock market is always subject to change. The idea of a pie chart allowing a retirement plan investor to "set it and forget it" is dangerous to your future retirement life.

You need to go back only as far as the examples in this book in Chapter One. Look at the investment results of the average retirement plan participant since 2000. These retirement plan participants made the two biggest mistakes that stock market investors can ever make:

1. They tried to argue with the stock market. That is, every stock market investor wants the stock market to continue to go up. They want the value of their retirement plan to continue to rise well into the double digits every year.

2. They did not make the necessary adjustments when the rules of the current stock market game changed. When the stock market music stopped, they did not even look for a chair to sit down in.

You can use a pie chart for baseline guidance on how to allocate your retirement plan assets. But in the future, don't use this cosmetic retirement planning tool for any more than a "picture" of your current retirement plan account holdings.

The static asset allocation pie chart is evil. It is not evil in its concept, but certainly in its use by most retirement plan participants. It must not be part of how you manage your retirement plan assets in the future.

Begin to direct your retirement plan assets toward the best available mutual fund options in your retirement plan menu. This is the most basic level of the concept of asset allocation.

In order to do that, you have to have a working knowledge of the concepts in the following chapters. Let me give you a little hint of what is to come, and how your investment management confidence is about to undergo a huge boost.

Close your eyes and begin to think of yourself as the retirement plan investor that you would like to become, based on your available time, current knowledge and interest level. To help you with that, let me give you some of the necessary attributes you would need to be a better retirement plan investment manager.

First, you need to know if the stock market is allowing you to make money in your retirement plan, or if the stock market is trying to take money away from you in your retirement plan.

Next, you will need to know which mutual funds in your retirement plan menu are in favor in the current stock market environment. It may be Growth or it may be Value mutual funds. Or Small, Mid or Large Cap mutual funds. But it surely is not going to be what a computer predicts it will be.

CHAPTER SIX

Bullish Percent Concept

There are several individuals who have enabled stock market risk-managers like me to be able to use this important tool to benefit our clients. Ernest Staby invented the Bullish Percent concept back in the 1940's. In 1955, A.W. Cohen created the NYSE Bullish Percent. And in 1998, Dorsey, Wright & Associates, Inc. taught me how to use this tool to benefit my retirement plan advice clients.

I will give you all you need to know about Bullish Percents. If you invest in the stock market, would it be helpful to have a tool that answers the question, "Is the stock market going up, or is the stock market going down *right now?*" The Bullish Percent tool answers that question any time you want to pay attention to it.

A study at the University of Chicago and in the book *The Latent Statistical Structure of Securities Price Changes* by Benjamin F. King, the Bullish Percent concept is quantified. This information offers the fact that 75 to 80 percent of the risk involved in owning an individual stock (or in the case of a mutual fund--a collection of individual stocks) is related to the stock market and the individual stock market sector. Only 20% of the risk in owning an individual stock is related to that individual stock.

Translation: If the stock market is not rising, there is not much of a chance that you are going to increase the value of your retirement plan account. And when you have to manage a menu of mutual fund options in a retirement account, it is almost impossible to make money in a stock market that is not going higher.

Like other things in life that are great successes, maintaining and building the value of your retirement account takes a plan. The Bullish Percent is the place to begin that plan.

The concept of Bullish Percent is best introduced by how it is used in real-life. At one time or another, even if by mistake, you have watched all or part of an episode of the television show, "Who Wants to Be a Millionaire?" The premise of the "Who Wants to Be a Millionaire?" is that the contestants pick one of four answers to a trivia question.

The show gives each contestant three "lifelines." If the contestant becomes stumped on a question, they can use the lifelines to get help.

One lifeline is a "50-50", which takes away two of the possible answers, leaving one correct and one incorrect answer. Another lifeline is to "phone a friend" and see if they know the answer that you need. The last lifeline is to "poll the audience." This lifeline allows the audience to guess at the right answer and then a computer displays what percentage of the audience voted for each answer.

What the producers of this show have found is that when you a phone a friend for an answer they are right about 65% of the time. When you poll the audience however, they are right 91% of the time.

This makes sense if you really think about it. Similarly, you're more likely to arrive at the right answer after polling a diverse group of people from all walks of life, educational and economic backgrounds, than from a small group of supposedly "smart" people that happen to be seen or quoted in the financial media promoting their financial perspectives.

The Bullish Percent tool that is available in Point & Figure charting is like "polling the audience" in the Millionaire show. The large and diverse sampling of both the large and small investors that have chosen at any time to allocate their investment resources in the stock market, will give you the most accurate picture available of the risk in owning stocks.

What you can see with the Bullish Percents is that this tool is better at assessing risk in the stock market than marketing material from an investment professional "talking head" on financial TV or interviewed in the financial print media.

At the end of each business day, the Bullish Percent "polls the audience." This audience is composed of about 3,000 stocks listed on both the New York Stock Exchange and NASDAQ. It is better at assessing risk than any tool that has been invented.

One of the best things about the Bullish Percent concept is that it is so simple to understand and follow. The only thing you need to remember about a Bullish Percent chart is the following two rules:

When the Bullish Percent chart is in X's, a retirement plan investor is in **Wealth Accumulation Mode.**

When the Bullish Percent chart is in O's, a retirement plan investor is in **Wealth Preservation Mode**.

If you remember the two rules mentioned above, you will have all you need to know about how to better manage the stock market risk in your retirement plan investing. If you add a little historical perspective to the charts and look at the extremely high levels and extremely low levels, you will be in select company as an effective stock market risk manager.

The main tools available to analyze the stock market risk environment are the NYSE Bullish Percent for NYSE stocks, and OTC Bullish Percent for NASDAQ stocks. These indicators work the same; they just analyze stocks on each exchange.

I played Division I football at the University of Minnesota. That is not an important stock market tool to know about, but the reason I mention it is that I know a lot about X's and O's and how important the symbols are to create meaning from data.

In a football game, two sides operate on the field at the same time. One team is on offense (X's) and the other team is on defense (O's).

Let me ask you here to think about the stock market in the same way. There are times when an investor in the stock market has the football and the offensive team is on the field. On offense, a stock market investor is trying to score as many points as possible because that is the time that the stock market is supporting higher prices. That would be noted by a column of X's on the Bullish Percent chart.

Just as there is an ebb and flow in a football game, the same natural action occurs in the stock market. There are times when the stock market is not supporting higher prices. As a stock market investor, you have lost the ball and must put the defensive team on the field. During such periods, the stock market is trying to score on you---that is, the stock market is trying to take as much money away from you as possible.

Take this analogy one step farther, and relate it to your favorite football team. How would they fare if they played the entire game with the offensive team on the field? They might do well when they had possession of the ball, but when the opposing team had the ball, your team would be scored on at will.

This is the problem most investors have: they don't know which team is on the field. To compound the problem, the financial media always thinks that the offensive team is on the field. And it is apparent in their poor stock market investment returns.

The main point here is that the Bullish Percent clearly signals when the stock market environment is supporting an offensive or defensive strategy for a retirement plan investor.

ATTRIBUTES OF A BULLISH PERCENT CHART

The NYSE Bullish Percent is simply a compilation of the percent of stocks that trade on the NYSE on Point and Figure buy signals. If you simply thumbed through all the Point and Figure chart patterns of the stocks on the NYSE and counted the ones that were on buy signals, and then divided by the total number of stocks evaluated, you would have the NYSE Bullish Percent reading.

Like we discussed in the previous chapter, here is a picture of a buy signal. In this picture to the right, the price of the stock has gone to a certain level, and then gone back down. Soon the

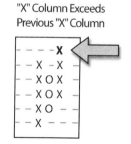

"X" Column Exceeds
Previous "X" Column

stock price rises to the same level, but this time the stock price goes through the level of previous resistance and moves to a higher price.

This is called a "double top break" on a Point & Figure chart. When a stock on the NYSE or NASDAQ records a similar chart pattern, that stock is then on a BUY signal and is counted in the percentage of stocks in that universe on a BUY signal. And that stock is added to the Bullish Percent.

Let's say for instance, there were 2,000 stocks on the NYSE and 1,000 of them were on Point and Figure buy signals. The Bullish Percent would be at 50% (1,000/2,000 = 50 percent).

The Bullish Percent concept is unique from most market indicators because it is a one stock - one vote indicator. Once a stock is on a BUY signal, that stock is always on a BUY signal, until it moves to a SELL signal like the picture below:

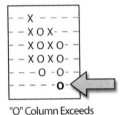

"O" Column Exceeds
Previous "O" Column

A stock on the NYSE or NASDAQ is either on a BUY signal or a SELL (sell signal example to left) signal at all times. In addition, a stock is only counted once in the calculation. The stock can move in price from $50 to $100; it only is counted as one BUY signal on that stock exchange.

Thus, the Bullish Percent concept is a measurement of the amount of participation in the stock market and its direction. It tells you if the market, sector or asset class is participating in an upward or downward movement. It is not an opinion. It is fact.

There are times when the market is supporting higher prices and times when the market is not supporting higher prices. The problem is that most stock market investors make the same mistakes during down market cycles--they buy stocks and mutual funds and hold them through the down cycles.

Here is the final piece of information you need to know for the calculation of the Bullish Percent for the NYSE or the NASDAQ. Let's use that same example of 2,000 stocks trading on the NYSE. Over the next week, 12 stocks experience a new buy signal and 10 stocks experience new sell signals.

The net result of the action for the week is two new buy signals. Thus two percent more stocks on the NYSE are on buy signals. Each box on the chart represents two percent, so a two percent net change in new buy signals allows the chart to raise one box.

The only way to switch from one column to the next is through a three-box reversal. It would take a sum total of six percent net buy or sell signals to cause a reversal. The box size is two percent and therefore a three box is a six percent move in either direction.

Reversing from one column to the next is tantamount to losing or gaining possession of "the football."

The Bullish Percent chart even looks a lot like a football field. The "playing field" runs from 0 to 100 percent. Where you are on that field determines your "field" position. The column you are in tells you if you have the football and the field position tells you how much room you have to run.

When you are in the Green Zone, below 30% and in a column of X's, you have a lot of room to run the ball. When you are in the Red Zone and in a column of O's, you have a lot of territory and you can lose the ball.

When the Bullish Percent goes near/below 30%, the availability of supply to continue to push the market lower is severely limited. All the stock market investors who want to sell their stocks have already sold them. When the Bullish Percent goes near/above the 70% level, the availability of demand to continue to push the market higher is severely limited. Everyone who wants to own stocks has already bought them. And they don't have any more money to spend.

That is all there is to it.

The Bullish Percent tool is all about knowing when to be offensive in X's for **Wealth Accumulation**, and knowing when to be defensive in O's for **Wealth Preservation**.

You should be excited that you know about this concept. If you realized how few stock market investors, both professional and amateur, know about this concept, you would not be able to sleep for the next several nights.

Bullish Percent Chart

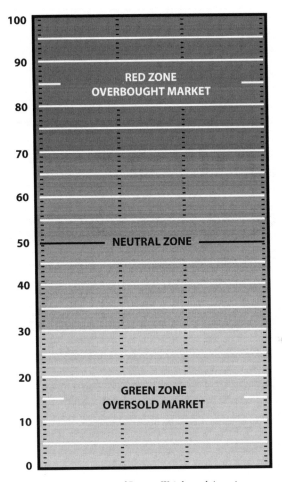

Chart courtesy of Dorsey Wright and Associates
(A color chart is available in the Chart Examples section
at the end of the book.).

Note: In the color version of the Bullish Percent Chart the
Red   =   Overbought, above 70%.
Neutral =   Middle of the field, between 30 and 70%
Green   =   Oversold, below 30%.

CHAPTER
seven
Sector and Asset Class Tools

Sector analysis is one of the most important aspects of the market. You might not understand why because you have probably never read a financial media article on the importance of sectors, or heard an expert talk about this information on financial TV.

This is about the only part of the equation that the financial media gets right. I am sure you have heard or read the following summary of the previous day's stock market trading, "Today the markets moved higher lead by good earnings reports in the technology stocks..."

All day every day, the financial media feeds the investing public's obsession of trying to pick the right stocks to own. In both television and print, there is a constant list of reasons why now is the perfect time to buy this stock or that stock. It seems like everyone has a reason for an investor to own his favorite stock.

But that information does not help a retirement plan investor who has to make decisions on a fixed menu of mutual fund options. Chances are that "everyone's favorite stock" is not even part of a mutual fund portfolio they could own.

A better use of a retirement plan investor's time is to use the tools that are available to help them make better decisions on not only "what to buy," but also "when to buy."

EXPANDING THE BULLISH PERCENT CONCEPT

The same principles used with the stock market bullish percent charts apply to the Sector Bullish percents. And the same principles used with the Sector Bullish Percents apply to mutual fund asset classes. So as a quick review, remember that the Bullish Percent concept can apply to stock market sectors and mutual fund asset classes.

Source: Morningstar

By ERISA law, a retirement plan menu of mutual fund options includes most of the assets classes in the matrix on the right.

There is no huge revelation here. The point is that you can track mutual fund asset classes the same way that you track stock market sectors. The most accurate way to do that is with the Bullish Percent concept.

So, as an example, if you want to know the "field position" of the Large Cap Value mutual fund asset class, you would just look at the Bullish Percent chart for that asset class of mutual funds. The Bullish Percent reading of all available Large Cap Value mutual funds would calculate the percentage of those specific mutual funds on a Point & Figure buy signal.

The Bullish Percent tool for mutual fund asset classes is especially helpful in determining the timing of adding new money to current holdings in your retirement plan. You would be hesitant to add new money to a mutual fund located in an asset class that clearly shows that class of mutual funds producing more and more sell signals.

ASSET CLASS BELL CURVE

In my retirement plan advice practice, I am always looking for ways to show my clients a "picture" of the current risk level of the stock market sectors and asset classes. And then I compare the current picture to historical ones. On the next page are two pictures of the mutual fund asset classes at extremely high and extremely low levels.

Each mutual fund asset class is assigned a symbol, and the Bullish Percent calculation of each mutual fund asset class is then plotted on a bell curve. The result is a "picture" of the risk level of all of the mutual fund asset classes.

The asset classes in lower case letters indicate that the Bullish Percent chart for that asset class is in O's and is moving to the left-hand side of the bell curve---or that there are more and more mutual funds in that asset class that are moving from a buy to a sell signal.

The asset classes in upper case letters indicate that the Bullish Percent for that asset class is in X's and is moving to the right-hand side of the curve---or that there are more and more mutual funds in that asset class that are moving to buy signals.

The most important aspect of the asset class bell curve is the "picture" it relates to you as the viewer. The most important thing to take away from viewing the asset class bell curve is whether the mutual fund asset classes are oversold, normally distributed, or overbought.

This is the same concept that you learned in your Statistics 101 class. Remember that 66% of the time the subject will remain within one standard deviation above or below the middle of the curve. When this measurement gets too far to the left or to the right, eventually it will come back to rest towards the middle of the curve.

As in Example 3A, you can view as a low-risk environment on the left-hand side of the curve and high risk environment on the right-hand side of the curve. Acceptable risk is the middle of the curve and lower.

Here's a list of characteristics found at the two extreme levels of the Asset Class Bell Curve.

Characteristics Found at the Low Risk Side of the Curve (left side)

EXAMPLE 3A

FROM OCTOBER 20, 2000

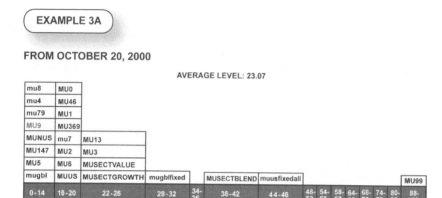

AVERAGE LEVEL: 23.07

mu8	MU0													
mu4	MU46													
mu79	MU1													
MU9	MU369													
MUNUS	mu7	MU13												
MU147	MU2	MU3												
MU5	MU6	MUSECTVALUE												
mugbl	MUUS	MUSECTGROWTH	mugblfixed		MUSECTBLEND	muusfixedall								MU99
0-14	16-20	22-26	28-32	34-36	38-42	44-46	48-52	54-56	58-62	64-66	68-72	74-78	80-86	88-100

Table courtesy of Dorsey Wright and Associates

Asset Class Bullish Percents in general have good field position. The stock market is undervalued and is at a low risk level.

NYSE and NASDAQ Bullish Percents are in O's signifying the stock markets are "washed out." All the sellers have already sold their stock.

Characteristics Found at the High Risk Side of the Curve (right side)

EXAMPLE 3B

FROM JANUARY 15, 2005

AVERAGE LEVEL: 90.59

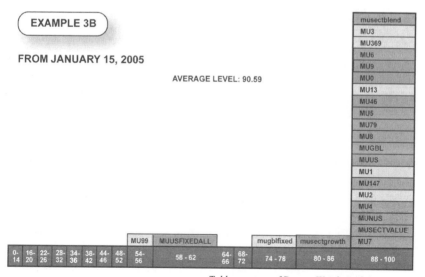

0-14	16-20	22-26	28-32	34-36	38-42	44-46	48-52	54-56			58-62	64-66	68-72	74-78	80-86	88-100
									MU99	MUUSFIXEDALL				mugblfixed	musectgrowth	MU7

(vertical column, top to bottom): musectblend, MU3, MU369, MU6, MU9, MU0, MU13, MU46, MU5, MU79, MU8, MUGBL, MUUS, MU1, MU147, MU2, MU4, MUNUS, MUSECTVALUE, MU7

Table courtesy of Dorsey Wright and Associates

Asset Class Bullish Percents in general have poor field position. The stock market is overvalued and is at a high risk level.

NYSE and NASDAQ Bullish Percents are in X's signifying the stock markets are "over bought." Everyone who wants to own stocks has bought them and there is probably not much new demand available to move stocks higher.

Let me run through a brief scenario to illustrate how this type of statistical representation can be useful. This statistical analysis stuff can get a little confusing sometimes, but I do want to discuss it because it is another tool that can help you make better decisions in the management of your retirement plan account.

Assume the stock market is in a buy mode. The NYSE Bullish Percent has just reversed up into X's from a low level and it has great field position. At the same time, there is a mutual fund asset class that has gone below 30% on its Bullish Percent chart, and has also reversed up into X's. By all accounts, this situation shapes up as a good buying opportunity.

Next, we have a found a mutual fund option in your retirement plan menu that has maintained its price in the stock market pullback. This mutual fund is in the above-mentioned asset class that is moving higher. This mutual fund has a strong chart pattern. Lastly, to put the icing on the cake, the bell curve shows both the asset class and the individual mutual fund on the left (oversold) side of the bell curve.

The above analysis of the situation took maybe a couple of minutes. Do you see the confidence you have in making the decision to place a portion of your retirement plan balance in this mutual fund? The above analysis never means that you can "set it and forget it," but wouldn't you feel better to be empowered to make this investment decision in the first place?

The rest of the retirement plan participant world operates in the stock market every day totally blind to this checklist of information. These investors, including the professional money managers that you hire to manage your retirement plan money, are always fully invested in the hope that the stock market continues to rise.

You now are on your way to understanding and working with these stock market risk barometers that will help you make better investment decisions in the management of your retirement plan account.

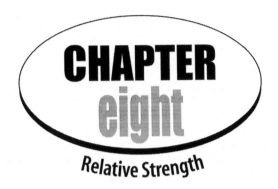

CHAPTER eight

Relative Strength

Do you know which mutual fund options are the best performers in your retirement plan menu? You would always know the answer to that question if you understood the importance of Relative Strength. Relative Strength measures how one mutual fund option in your retirement plan menu is performing compared to another option available to you. It also measures how each mutual fund option in your retirement plan menu is performing as compared to a popular stock market index like the S&P 500 or the Russell 2000.

Relative Strength is the investment performance tool that answers the most basic questions that every retirement plan participant has at any point in time, about any mutual fund position he or she currently owns. That is, "Am I in the right mutual fund at the right time, or am I in the wrong mutual fund at the wrong time?"

The best attribute about Relative Strength, is that it has no bias. Used correctly and continuously, Relative Strength will keep you in the right mutual fund options in your retirement plan. More importantly, it will keep you out of the wrong mutual fund options in your retirement plan.

The behavioral changes that are needed to improve the investment performance in the management of your retirement plan begin with the knowledge and use of Relative Strength. The most unbiased and unemotional stock market performance tool ever invented is Relative Strength.

Retirement plan investors make the same mistakes, year after year, in the management of their retirement plans. Their biggest mistake is continuing to operate without a logical and organized method of analyzing the mutual fund options available to them. These investors attempt to make money in stock markets that are clearly configured to take money away from them. In short, these investors continue to argue with the stock market over the direction it wants to move.

The main reason to use Relative Strength is that it has no bias. It is a measurement that tells a mutual fund's performance exactly how it is. It gives you the best information on performance so that you can make a more informed decision.

As I am sure you know, sooner or later, you have to make a choice in your retirement plan as to which mutual funds you want to own. And you must know why you want to own them. Then a little while later you have to decide if you want to continue to own the same mutual funds, or exchange them for other mutual fund options. If that is not enough of a challenge, you eventually have to decide when to sell your holdings in this mutual fund.

Relative Strength will help make all those vitally important risk-management decisions easy for you. The reason is that Relative Strength is another important investment management tool that will give you the right answer to all of the above retirement plan portfolio management questions.

Let me just summarize the importance of Relative Strength, and why you absolutely have to use it to manage your retirement plan assets.

- If you want to know if you are invested in the best possible mutual fund options available in your retirement plan menu, then you have to use Relative Strength.

- If you want to know which mutual fund options in your retirement plan menu are beginning to outperform other options in your retirement plan menu, then you have to use Relative Strength.

- If you want to know which mutual fund options in your retirement plan menu are beginning to underperform other options in your retirement plan menu, then you have to use

Relative Strength.

- If you want to know which mutual fund options in your retirement plan menu have outperformed other mutual fund options in your retirement plan menu, over the long-term in both up markets and down markets, then you have to use Relative Strength.

TYING TOGETHER BULLISH PERCENT AND RELATIVE STRENGTH

If you wanted to go sailing today, you would want to know how hard the wind is blowing and from what direction it is blowing. These measurements can change, even on the same day, but you at least want to know that information when you start out on your sailing trip. And you would want to make the necessary adjustments during your sailing trip.

The Point & Figure tool that tells you what direction the wind is blowing is the Bullish Percent. It will show you very clearly the mutual fund assets classes that are beginning to move up or down in price, and at what level of risk the current movement is. Any time you look at a Bullish Percent chart on a stock market exchange or a mutual fund asset class, that information is available.

The Point & Figure indicator that will tell you hard the wind is blowing is Relative Strength. These charts tell you the magnitude of participation in a trend. The Relative Strength chart will tell you the magnitude of participation of a mutual fund versus the upward or downward movement in the stock market or asset class.

Relative Strength tells you whether the long-term trend of a mutual fund option in your retirement plan menu has been up or down. And if that trend is more or less likely to continue.

Relative Strength will keep your mutual fund holdings in sync with the way the markets and asset classes are moving. Knowledge of Relative Strength will allow you to own the mutual fund options in your retirement plan that are outperforming, and avoid the mutual funds that are underperforming.

At the most basic level of how you manage your retirement plan assets, ask yourself these two questions:

If I am going to take the risk associated with owning stock market mutual funds, wouldn't it make sense for me to own the mutual funds in my retirement plan menu that are going up in value at as fast a rate--or even faster--than the S&P 500?

Conversely, wouldn't it also make sense NOT to own the mutual funds in my retirement plan menu that are going down in value at a faster rate--or faster--than the S&P 500?

Again, the answers to those two questions are found with the Relative Strength tool.

MEASURING RELATIVE STRENGTH

There are two ways to measure the performance (or underperformance) of a mutual fund. The first measurement of Relative Strength is to measure the performance of the mutual fund versus the overall market. In my retirement plan advice work, I measure performance or underperformance versus the S&P 500 Equal-Weighted Index.

The S&P Equal Dollar Weighted Index is, as its name implies, equal dollar weighted. This benchmark tool provides a clear picture of the broad market, not just a handful of the largest stocks in an index, like the S&P 500 Index.

Calculating the Relative Strength is performed at the end of every business day, and the result is plotted on a Point & Figure chart.

The second measurement of Relative Strength is to measure the performance of your mutual fund to other mutual funds of the same class (Large, Mid or Small Cap) or style (Value, Growth or Blend.). As an example, you would measure a Large Cap Value mutual fund option available in your retirement plan menu relative to all the other Large Cap Value mutual funds available.

This Relative Strength measurement is calculated the same way as the first. It allows you to identify the mutual funds available in your retirement plan that are the "best of the best." These mutual funds are measured against all of your retirement plan mutual fund options, as well as all mutual funds available to investors.

Relative Strength is an extremely important concept to understand because both stocks and mutual funds with strong Relative Strength will typically outperform the S&P 500 in an up stock market, and will be much more likely to hold up better in a down stock market.

WHAT A RELATIVE STRENGTH CHART IS TELLING YOU...IF YOU WANT TO LISTEN

Relative Strength charts look the same as the Bullish Percent charts we talked about in Chapter Three. But, they are read a little bit differently.

On a Relative Strength chart, we are primarily interested in signals and columns. The patterns of interest are simply double top breaks and double bottom breaks. This identifies whether the Relative Strength chart is positive (on a buy signal/ double top) or negative (on a sell signal/ double bottom).

The column is also important to a Relative Strength chart. If the chart is in X's, it shows that the mutual fund is outperforming the S&P

500 in the short term. If the chart is in Os, then the mutual fund is underperforming the S&P 500 in the short term.

A column of X's on a Relative Strength chart suggests that the mutual fund in question will outperform the S&P 500. A column of O's on the Relative Strength chart suggests that the same mutual fund will under perform the S&P 500.

Here is a simple question for you. It is designed to take a mental break from all of this technical data.

If you are going to take the risks associated with owning stocks and owning mutual funds that own stocks in your retirement plan, does it make sense to use a tool that will tell you if you are invested in the right mutual funds?

I think your answer to that question would be "yes." I mean that is what the stock market game is all about. If you take the risks, you should at least get a return that is equal to or hopefully better than "the market." Relative Strength will help you better manage the decision on what mutual fund you should buy and own.

Also know that that Relative Strength signals are long-term in nature. Typically a Relative Strength signal will last for roughly 1.5 to 2 years.

- Below is a quick summary of the four Relative Strength conditions possible for an individual mutual fund. These conditions move from the strongest performer to the weakest performer.

- Relative Strength chart is on a buy signal and in a column of X's. This is the strongest reading possible for a Relative Strength chart. The buy signal shows the mutual fund outperforming the S&P 500 over the long-term, and over the short-term. This is the best possible case for mutual fund performance.

- Relative Strength on a buy signal and in a column of O's. This condition demonstrates that the mutual fund is outperforming on a longer-term basis, but is currently "taking a rest." As long as the Relative Strength chart remains on a buy signal, the Relative Strength is intact.

- Relative Strength on a Sell signal in X's. In this case, the mutual fund has been underperforming the S&P 500. However, the reversal to X's indicates that on a short-term basis, it is managing to show strength.

- Relative Strength on a sell signal in O's. This is the weakest status of the four. This indicates that the mutual fund is significantly underperforming the S&P 500 and the recent action by the fund shows that it continues to under perform the index.

In my communications with my retirement plan advice clients, I provide a summary of the above information. I realized early in my retirement plan advice career, that my clients were too busy to find and monitor Relative Strength on their own. So, I summarize it for them in the following way:

Each of the above Relative Strength conditions is assigned one point. Mutual funds that have three or more of the above Relative Strength conditions are considered strong mutual funds to own. Mutual funds that earn only two or less points are not considered quality mutual funds to own at any time.

Remember that Relative Strength does not help determine price direction of a mutual fund. If the S&P 500 falls 10% and the mutual fund you own falls 5%, it has demonstrated positive Relative Strength.

If you hope to outperform the overall stock market, the only way to do so is to be invested in stocks and mutual funds that have positive Relative Strength.

A DIFFERENT USE OF RELATIVE STRENGTH

You can also use Relative Strength in a different way. I provide this investment advisory review when I first sit down with a prospective client. As we have discussed earlier, the typical retirement plan participant is over-weighted in the Large Cap mutual fund options available to them. Again, this is no fault of theirs; it is just the way the retirement plan world works.

Relative Strength will allow you to take a hard look at your current mutual fund holdings in your retirement plan. If you currently own some funds that have not kept up as the stock market has moved higher, it would be time to sell them. As we learned in Chapter Six on Bullish Percents, when the stock market indicators show that the demand is beginning to dry up and supply is beginning to take over, you can then use the Relative Strength tools to show you which mutual funds should be sold first.

The mutual funds in your retirement plan menu whose performance has lagged the overall stock market in an upward move are the same mutual funds that went down at a faster rate when the stock markets declined. Also, these poor performers are not likely to hold up as well if the stock markets move lower. You should not own poor Relative Strength mutual funds when the Bullish Percents are at high levels and begin to move down.

In the early stages of a stock market decline, Relative Strength measurements are critical. If the mutual funds you own have not kept up with the S&P 500 or mutual fund peers (in the same asset class) while the market headed higher, they are not likely to hold up well as the market moves lower. Relative Strength is the best tool to use to help you determine which mutual funds get sold and which are held as the risk in the stock market increases.

When the Bullish Percents suggest a more defensive posture, the most sensible approach in the early stages of a declining stock market is to sell off the mutual funds you own that have poor Relative Strength and put the proceeds from those sales in your retirement plan money market. Removing these mutual funds from your retirement plan portfolio won't hurt your performance and it will preserve your principal value. You can then hold on to your strong Relative Strength performers because they will hold up better in a stock market decline.

Strong Relative Strength performers will come back faster when the market moves as well. And because you have a money market balance built up in your retirement plan money market, you will be able to buy more of the strong Relative Strength mutual funds available in your retirement plan when the OFFENSE comes back on to the stock market field.

The proper use of Relative Strength does two things for your retirement plan. First, it raises the cash balance in your retirement plan so your retirement plan is more resistant to a potential stock market decline. And second, the mutual funds that you continue to own in your retirement plan will most likely continue to outperform the S&P 500--- both if the stock market goes down, or goes higher. Three key notions have been advanced:

- Keep underperforming mutual funds out of your portfolio.

- Only stay invested in mutual funds that outperform the S&P 500.

- As mutual funds lose Relative Strength, build up your money market balance.

CHAPTER
nine
Relative Strength Examples

This chapter is for the overwhelmed. If you feel like all this information is a bit too much like being told how to build the watch when you really just want to know the time of day, then this is the best chapter of this book to read. If you can make it to the end of this chapter, and believe what I am telling you about Relative Strength, then you will be set to properly manage your retirement plan account.

Do you remember the part earlier in the book when I said that the buy-and-hold investment management posture for your retirement account was a bad thing? I meant every word of it. But there is one way to buy-and-hold that will make you a successful retirement plan investor. That is to buy-and-hold your retirement plan mutual funds that have strong Relative Strength.

I have nothing against the theory of buy-and-hold investing if it makes adjustments to the current realities of the stock market. Again, I realize that some retirement plan investors just don't have the time necessary to monitor the investments in their retirement plans. In reality, many of those busy professionals are clients of mine. They pay me to watch things for them and to help them make better decisions on the few occasions every year when I draw their attention to their retirement plans.

I also realize that there are retirement plan investors that just don't have the interest in paying attention to their retirement plan. I have clients like this also. Try as they might to be fully aware that everything they read and hear says that they should pay more attention to the largest part of their investment net worth, they just can't do it.

This chapter is to let those two types of retirement plan investors know that I understand. I really do. It is OK if they buy-and-hold their retirement plan investments both now and in the future. But they must promise me (or pay my advisory fees) to use the Relative Strength tools to understand WHEN they should buy-and-hold.

If you are aware of the underperformance and out performance of each mutual fund option in your retirement plan menu, then you are OK to buy-and-hold. That is how powerful and important the Relative Strength tool is.

The same thing goes for investment professionals. Many of the professionals that I teach about retirement plan risk-management are concerned that they don't really understand exactly how to provide this advice.

An investment professional, as well as an individual investor, will not go too far wrong in the management of any retirement plan assets, if he or she simply follows the Relative Strength principles.

If you are starved for the time, suffer from a lack of interest, or just want to pay a professional to do it for you, as long as you know that professional has a deep understanding of Relative Strength, you will avoid a retirement plan disaster.

RELATIVE STRENGTH EXAMPLE

The Relative Strength chart of the SML (The Standard & Poor's Small Cap 600 Index) versus the S&P 500 reversed up into a column of X's on 2-17-2000. This index is a good proxy for the Small Cap style of mutual funds. There has not been a time since then that the Relative Strength of the Small Cap style of mutual funds has wavered or lagged the overall stock market as measured by the S&P 500 Index.

Even during the period from mid February of 2000 until I write this information in May of 2005, Small Cap stock mutual funds have both outperformed the S&P 500 on the upside when that index has gone up, and gone down at a slower rate than the S&P 500 on the downside when that index has gone down.

The same thing can be said of the Standard & Poor's Mid-Cap 400 Depositary Receipt, which can be used as a good proxy for the Mid Cap style of mutual funds. The security holds all of the S&P stocks in the Mid Cap 400 Index. It reversed up on its Relative Strength chart versus the S&P 500 on 9-12-2000. And like its Small Cap cousin, it has not looked back since that time.

So the point of this part of the discussion on Relative Strength is that it is one of the few investment management tools that can be used for a buy-and-hold investment management posture. The key is that you, or the advisor you work with, has to know if the Relative Strength is in your favor when you buy the mutual fund, and if the Relative Strength stays in your favor during the time you own the mutual fund. And of course, you should sell the mutual fund as soon as Relative Strength leaves that asset.

CHAPTER
ten

Putting it All Together

As we begin this chapter, let's summarize what we have learned:

- The stock market game is all about supply and demand. There is nothing else that you will ever hear or see from the financial media that will be more important to your financial future than that information.

- The financial media is not your friend. Pay little attention to any stock market information they produce. I also have suspicions about your retirement plan provider (the company that has custody of your retirement plan assets) and your retirement plan sponsor (your company). Maybe I should write a book about that?

- You have to know (as part of your investment management tools) if the stock market is currently configured to **Accumulate Wealth** in your retirement plan, or if you are better off in a **Wealth Preservation Mode**. The Bullish Percents will give you that information.

- It is much easier to make a decision on which mutual fund options to own in your retirement plan if you are aware of and use the Relative Strength measurement tools. Those tools make it so much easier to know "what to own" and "what not to own."

- You now can use the Bullish Percent tools to monitor the availability of demand in both the stock market and a mutual fund asset class. You can now use the Relative Strength tools to confirm where to both invest and not invest the money in your retirement plan account.

- You have to, for the sake of your retirement future, change the way you manage the money in your retirement plan. The tools are there, and now you have at least a partial explanation of how they work and how to use them.

You now know what strategy to use (**Wealth Accumulation** or **Wealth Preservation**), what specific asset classes to look at (Bullish Percents), and which specific mutual funds should be on your team (Relative Strength). What else is there to know?

I think it would be helpful now to set up a checklist of the steps involved in using the Point & Figure tools to manage your retirement plan.

✓**1:** Evaluate the Condition of the Stock Market Are You in Principal Preservation or Principal Accumulation Mode?

We first take a look at the NYSE Bullish Percent and notice which column this indicator is in and what is the field position. This "picture" will determine the first level of our **Wealth Accumulation** or **Wealth Preservation** plan.

We should look at the same Bullish Percent indicator for the S&P 500 because of the importance those 500 stocks play in the performance of the vast majority of mutual fund options in your retirement plan. Again, notice the column this indicator is in and what the field position is.

The last stop on the first level of the Game Plan is the Bullish Percent for the MU100. This is a Dorsey, Wright & Associates, Inc. mutual fund indicator that can be accessed at the Dorsey, Wright & Associates, Inc. Web site (www.dorseywright.com). This indicator gives a clear picture of the risk level for the 100 most-widely owned stocks in the mutual fund world at the end of every calendar quarter. Again, watch the column and field position.

√2: If you are in WEALTH ACCUMULATION mode…Do You
Want to Own Large Cap, Mid Cap or Small Cap?

You often hear companies or different mutual funds being
categorized as "small-cap," "mid-cap," or "large-cap." The word "cap" is
short for capitalization, which is a measure that can classify a company's
size. Small Cap refers to stocks with a market capitalization between
$300 million to $2 billion. Mid Cap is short for "Middle Cap," and refers
to stocks with a market capitalization of between $2 billion to $10 billion.
Large Cap companies typically have a market capitalization between $10
billion and $200 billion.

Now that you know why some of the mutual fund options in your
retirement plan are categorized according to market capitalization, you
can just as quickly forget it. Market Cap is just a name to put the mutual
fund options available in your retirement plan in categories that are
supposed to help you keep things straight. But they don't.

The only good news is that market capitalizations have Bullish
Percent charts. They will allow you to assess the risk level of each class
of mutual fund, and make an intelligent decision on the risk level you are
willing to take in owning that type of mutual fund.

Next, Relative Strength comes into your retirement plan investment
management life again. Remember that we are looking for under
performance and out performance of the mutual funds available to you.
Start looking at the Relative Strength charts of each class of mutual fund
as compared to the performance of the S&P 500.

The Standard & Poor's SmallCap 600 Index is a capitalization-
weighted index that measures the performance of selected U.S. stocks
with a small market capitalization. This security is a good proxy for the
Small Cap style of mutual funds.

The Standard & Poor's Mid-Cap 400 Depositary Receipt is a good
proxy for the Mid Cap style of mutual funds. It is designed to generally
correspond to the performance of the S&P MidCap 400 Index. The fund
holds all of the S&P stocks in the MidCap 400 Index.

Both of the above proxies can be compared to the Relative Strength
of the S&P 500 both short and long-term in order to determine which
market capitalization class of mutual funds would be the best to own in
retirement plan at a given time.

Think about mutual fund asset class Relative Strength in the same terms of when you go to Dairy Queen and order an ice cream cone. Your options are small, medium or large ice cream cones. One of those sizes of cones will fit your appetite. Similarly, with mutual fund classifications, one of those classes has to be performing better than the other two and thus better fits your investment appetite. The class that you clearly see is outperforming the other two is where you want to put most of the money in your retirement plan.

✓**3:** Still in WEALTH ACCUMULATION Mode?
Do You Want to Own Value, Growth or International stocks?

Value and growth are two different investing styles used by mutual fund managers.

These are just more confusing descriptions common to the investment world. Like most things on your retirement plan provider Web site, the content is not intended to help you. The content is intended to fill up the pages.

Value mutual funds primarily hold stocks that are deemed to be undervalued in price. Every menu of options in a retirement plan has a value fund component, which is often broken down by size. For example, there may be one or all of a small-, mid- and large-cap value fund in your retirement plan menu.

Most growth mutual funds own stock in companies that reinvest their earnings into expansion, acquisitions, and/or research and development. Historically, growth funds offer higher potential growth, but usually at a higher risk.

If you can remember back to March of 2000 again, the Growth stocks (specifically growth technology stocks) were the stocks responsible for the high-water mark in your retirement plan. Also remember that retirement plan investors had no way of knowing when growth stocks went "out of favor" with large institutional investors.

A REAL-LIFE GROWTH VERSUS VALUE DISASTER

I have run into this specific situation, or a slight variation of it, many times in meeting with retirement plan investors over the last few years. I am not going to "change the name to protect the innocent," because no one involved in this mess was innocent. Except maybe the unfortunate retirement plan participant.

I have nothing good or bad to say about the Vanguard mutual fund family. The truth is, I don't care either way. I run into their mutual funds frequently with some of the retirement plan menus I monitor for my retirement plan advice clients. For that reason, I am familiar with these details.

The main character in this story is the Vanguard Value Index, whose ticker symbol is VIVAX. The story begins in October 2000. No retirement plan investors knew it at the time, but there was a very important stock market risk-management cycle in the early stages of development.

On October 2, 2000, the Relative Strength chart of the Vanguard Value Index reversed into a column of X's, when compared to the Vanguard Growth Index. Said another way, for the first time since May of 1997, the Vanguard Value mutual funds were poised to outperform the Vanguard Growth mutual funds.

Just a few days later, the Relative Strength chart of the Vanguard US Value Index, whose ticker symbol is VUVLX, was poised to outperform the Vanguard US Growth Index, whose ticker symbol is VWUSX. The reason I know that is because the Relative Strength chart reversed into a column of X's on 10-27-2000.

This second Relative Strength chart would act as a confirmation to the first set of events in this story. That is, that beginning in early October of 2000, US Value mutual funds were beginning to outperform US Growth mutual funds.

I know what you are thinking. First, why is that important? Second, who in the world would care about those two seemingly unimportant events? The answer to both questions is to go back and look at the price performance of these Vanguard mutual funds since October of 2000.

In the summer of 2000, the Vanguard Growth Index was doing just fine at $38 per share. I am sure that the retirement plan investors that were following their retirement plan provider's on-line Retirement Plan Tools were very happy with their previous investment returns. These investors had enjoyed several years of double-digit returns in their retirement plan, due to the over-weighting of Large Cap Growth mutual funds.

The problem was that in October 2000, the growth mutual funds stopped their several years of out performance over all other retirement plan menu options. I can't tell you the exact reason why it happened because I don't have to know why it happened. All I know is that in October of 2000, it did happen.

By the way, my retirement plan advice clients never care about WHY things happen. They pay me to alert them WHEN things happen, especially those things that will take money away from them in their retirement plans.

May 1997
Relative strength suggests Vanguard Value Index poised to underperform Vanguard Growth Index

October 2000
This double top buy signal suggests that for the first time in over 3 years, the Vanguard Value Index is poised to outperform the Vanguard Growth Index. This relative strength buy signal is still in play today.

```
                                        93.840
                                        90.886
                                        88.025
                                        85.255
                                        82.571
             |  |       | |      O       79.972
  1 |        X |       7   ----- 77.455
X O|        3 O 6   C   ----- 75.017
| O|        2 O 4 O 5  ----- 72.655
| 5|        1 A X O X         70.368
| 1|        X C X A X   ----- 68.153
| 6|        X 2   O |   ----- 66.008
| 7|        C |        |         63.930
| 8 6 |     X |
| O X O     B |
| C X O     X |
| 1 X 9    [A]
| 4     O 5    X |
| |    B 4 0 9 |
| |    O X O X |
| |    C X 6 X |
| |    2   O | |
| |    |       | |
| |    |       | |
| |    |       | |
```

Chart courtesy of Dorsey Wright & Associates

The retirement plan sponsor, the retirement plan provider, the on-line retirement plan tools and pie charts, and the Vanguard mutual fund company did not do one thing to alert retirement plan investors about this change in stock market leadership. That is because it is in the best interest of each of these entities for the retirement plan participant to remain fully invested in the buy-and-hold mode.

The Vanguard Growth Index closed in the $18 area in October of 2002. That is a decline from $38 to $18. That is a principal loss of 52.63%.

I will save you the trouble of looking back to chapter one and finding the "Get Your Money Back" formula. Here it is again:

Take the percent loss and divide by (100 minus the percent loss)

Investment down by ?% = **% return needed to**
(100 - % down)   **get back to even.**

Losing 52% of your retirement plan principal requires a return of 108% to get your money back.

As drastic as those numbers are in this example, they are not the main point of this story. The main point is that no one involved in the investment management of this retirement plan menu option notified the retirement plan participants that owned the Vanguard Growth Index of this major change of stock market risk.

The reason is that there was no logical reason to do that. The on-line retirement plan tools were looking great with their multi-colored pie charts. The asset allocation charts looked great as well. It was not the anniversary of the retirement plan participant using the on-line retirement planning tools. So there was no reason to think that there was anything wrong with over-weighting to Large Cap Growth mutual funds.

The retirement plan provider, retirement plan sponsor, and on-line retirement planning tools all failed the retirement plan participants in this story. These entities all kept the retirement plan participants over-exposed to Large Cap Growth mutual funds regardless of stock market conditions, because the computer-generated information gave no reason for changes to be made in a retirement plan investor's account.

Current stock market conditions are not even addressed by on-line retirement planning tools. That's because the tools have no mechanism to make the necessary changes to the current stock market reality.

To finish this story, let me interject another character in the same Vanguard mutual fund family. This mutual fund is most times a retirement plan investment option along with the Vanguard Growth Index. The name of this fund is the Vanguard Wellesley fund. The ticker symbol is VWINX.

The Relative Strength chart of VWINX reversed into X's versus the Vanguard Growth Index on 10-3-2002. This relative strength signal came right along the same time that Value was beginning to outperform Growth. This Vanguard Wellesley fund would have given you the same signal to move out of Growth mutual funds and into Value mutual funds.

The Vanguard Growth Index went down over 56% during the same time period that the Vanguard Wellesley fund went up from $15.50 in October of 2000 to $17.30 or so in October of 2002, a return of 10.40%.

The point of this story is that the tools are there for us to use. And if you know how to use them, or are working with an advisor that knows how to use them, they can make a dramatic difference in the performance of your retirement plan.

INTERNATIONAL FUNDS ARE RETIREMENT PLAN OPTIONS, TOO

The last category of stock mutual funds available in a retirement plan menu would be an International Stock Fund. This mutual fund can invest in companies located anywhere outside of the United States. You may also see reference made to a Global Equity Fund in your retirement plan menu. The difference is that a Global Fund includes the entire world, and an International Fund includes the entire world excluding your home country.

Again, there are Bullish Percents and Relative Strength measurements that are available to help sort out where to place your retirement plan money. Some useful indices to use to determine underperformance and out performance are the Russell 2000 Index which measures the performance of the 2,000 smallest companies in the Russell 3000 Index. The Russell 2000 serves as a benchmark for small-cap stocks in the United States.

Think in terms of managing the inventory of mutual funds available in your retirement plan. The best asset classes are indicated by the Bullish Percent charts that are in X's and in good field position. Next would be the best looking Relative Strength charts on each specific mutual fund that is in the best looking asset class.

After you set up your portfolio of mutual funds you want to own, it takes just a little bit of time to monitor your holdings. As the stock market and asset class Bullish Percents reverse into O's from high levels, you will want to sell the weakest Relative Strength mutual funds in your portfolio. Then take the proceeds from those sales and move to the safety of the money market until you can safely determine the best replacement asset class(s) to own.

CHAPTER eleven

You, Too, Can Have Your Own Investment Policy Statement

We have heard this all of our adult lives, and even before that when we were children in grade school. That is, "You have to have a plan in order to succeed." "Plan your work and work your plan."

The problem is that a plan takes time.

The other thing about having a plan is that if you have no idea what the plan should include, the plan will not be very good. That is the major problem I have seen for retirement plan participants' stock market investments. These retirement plan participants would be very happy to have a stock market game plan, but they are not sure how to get started or where to find the information.

In this chapter I am going to walk you through the same Investment Policy Statement that I use for many of my retirement plan participant clients. The following example will not be as detailed as the one I use, but it will be easy to understand and make sense to you.

The first thing you have to know is what an Investment Policy Statement is and what it is used for. An Investment Policy Statement is a document that will assist you (and if you choose to work with an advisor), in the supervision, monitoring and evaluating of the mutual fund options available to you in your retirement plan. This document states in writing your attitudes, expectations, objectives and guidelines to manage the mutual fund options in your retirement plan menu. It also sets the structure for managing your retirement plan account in accordance with your current investment objectives.

The first thing to do is to set a beginning valuation of your retirement plan on a specific date. You will find that this is an important psychological tool that will help you change your investment behavior as time progresses. When you see what a good job you will begin to do in the management of both your current retirement plan assets and your new contributions from both yourself and your employer, it will be a good motivator for you.

Next, state the objective you have for your retirement plan account. You don't have to get too fancy here. The simple objective of "having enough money to retire when I am age 60" will work just fine. The most important step here is to get some of these things down on paper and out-in-the-open with both you and your advisor.

As an example to get you started, I always disclose to my client that the first and foremost objective I have for providing them risk-management advice in their retirement plan account:

1. The primary investment objective is to PRESERVE THE PRINCIPAL VALUE of the assets in your retirement plan account.

2. The secondary investment objective is to GROW THE PRINCIPAL VALUE of the assets in your retirement plan account.

After you have read this far in this book, this may not seem like new information. You are in a small minority of retirement plan investors now. Not one retirement plan investor I have ever met with has looked at his or her retirement plan relative to these two investment objectives.

Now make a list of the investment principles you want to follow in the way you will begin to manage your retirement plan account. Put in writing the fact that with your new knowledge of the Point & Figure risk-management tools, you now realize that there are times when the stock markets are depressed and the risk is low, and there are times when the stock markets are extended and the risk is high.

What you want to acknowledge here is that going forward, you will make every attempt to strike a balance between participating in potential stock market upside and under-participating in potential stock market downside.

Next, state your time horizon for this Investment Policy Statement. The most logical choice would be your anticipated retirement date.

Also, establish the formal criteria to select, monitor, evaluate and compare the performance of the mutual fund options in your retirement plan menu on a regular basis. You can use with confidence your new stock market risk-management tools.

You have read earlier in this book about my use of the S&P 500 Index as a performance benchmark. You can pick any benchmark that you want. I use the S&P 500 because of its relevance to the structure of the mutual fund world. Remember that 75% of the stock market capitalization in the United States stock markets resides in the S&P 500.

Now comes probably the most important part of this document. That is the language about your tolerance for risk in the way you manage your retirement plan account.

State that you realize that with all stock market investments, there will be some short and intermediate term variability in investment returns. That kind of thing is just going to happen with stock market investments. But remember here, that you are now a smarter manager of stock market risk than when you started reading this book. Now is the time to put that reality in writing where you can go back and remind yourself when you need to do so.

I can't do any better job of explaining this concept than to just let you read what is included in my firm's Investment Policy Statement:

"The experience of Lager & Company, Inc. is that over a complete stock market cycle, it is much more important to manage the downside risk of the stock market than it is to show spectacular growth on the upside. The investment objective of Lager & Company, Inc. is to deliver consistent performance over time along with growth of capital with reasonable risk."

You are almost through the toughest part of this document now. This next part is "where the rubber meets the road." You have to name names and stick to your guns here.

Set your loss limits for each mutual fund position you own in your retirement plan account. That is, put in writing what you (and your advisor) agree to as to the dollar or percentage loss you are willing to tolerate when the stock market goes down.

Unfortunately, I can't help you much here. For what it is worth, I usually use a 10% loss limit for my clients. When you lose more than 10% in any single mutual fund position, it is clear that you own the mutual fund in the wrong kind of stock market or just at the wrong time in general. Or, you just own the wrong mutual fund.

This last part of "naming names" looks hard, but it is not. Insert into your document the return that you expect to get each investment year. This will be your target return percentage per year.

In this part of my firm's Investment Policy Statement, I always go back to the S&P 500 for the all the reasons stated previously. I explain it to my clients this way:

If you are going to take the risk associated with owning stock market investments, you have to set a benchmark to see how you are progressing once in a while. Because of the importance of the S&P 500 in the mutual fund investment world, that is our benchmark for a couple of important reasons.

First, we don't want to own any mutual fund options in your retirement plan menu that are not performing at least as well as the S&P 500 Index. We should sell any mutual fund option as soon as it begins to under perform this index. Going forward, there is just no reason to own any mutual fund that is not going up at least as much as, or more, than the S&P 500 Index.

Second, if the total return of your retirement plan account exceeds the return of the S&P 500 on an annual basis, then you know you are doing a good job of managing your account. If you are working with an advisor, then you can realize value in the advice that he or she is providing. And you can rest assured that you are gaining more in investment returns than you are paying in advisory fees every year.

One note of caution here: If you are working with an investment advisor, make sure that the annual returns numbers are reported on a relative basis. That is to say, make sure that the performance numbers are reported in the context of the performance of your benchmark.

Don't tolerate an investment advisor that reports to you that you outperformed your benchmark by "only declining 15% the previous year," when the benchmark was down 20% over the same period. That is not acceptable. If you manage your retirement plan account or if you work with an advisor, you are now too educated for those kind of investment returns. Go back and read Chapter One in order to be scared into seeing the importance of this fact.

That is about all you need to set up your Investment Policy Statement for your retirement plan account. It should just be a couple of pages at most. Again, it does not have to be complicated, it just has to work for how you want to manage and grow the value of your retirement plan account.

THINGS TO AVOID IN YOUR INVESTMENT POLICY STATEMENT

You can avoid just about anything you have read or heard about from the financial media in regard to "how you should manage your retirement plan money." This list includes the following financial buzzwords and nonsensical financial management concepts:

✓ PERIODIC REBALANCING

This is a good idea for the tires on your car (every 25-30,000 miles is best), but it makes no sense in the management of your retirement plan account.

You have learned that once your retirement plan account is "in sync" with the primary trend of the stock markets, there is not much to do. If you own the best available mutual funds you have access to in your retirement plan menu, and the primary trend of the stock markets is higher, you are in fine shape.

You can fine-tune the above situation with Relative Strength. As you now know, this tool will make sure you only own the best-performing mutual fund options available in your retirement plan menu.

And when the Relative Strength changes, you will change your current holdings along with it.

That is where the process should stop. You should not make a move in the management of your retirement plan account based on some arbitrary date--like the end of a calendar year or the anniversary of your account, or the date you were hired at your company, and for heavens sake, not the date you think you are going to retire. Those are dates that are necessary for computer programs, not for the way the stock market really works.

The second point to make on the topic of periodic rebalancing is the stupidity of selling a percentage of the best-performing mutual funds in your retirement plan account because of any of the arbitrary dates listed previously. Let me explain this ridiculous concept this way:

If you had 100% of your retirement plan account in the best-performing mutual fund option available to you in your retirement plan menu, would you sell it just because it was the beginning of January? Or because that mutual fund position represented too large a percentage of your retirement account value?

Maybe the example of a 100% position in one mutual fund is too extreme. But the experts that recommend periodic rebalancing are talking about the same concept. Sell part of what is working in your retirement plan account if it becomes too big a piece of your retirement plan account.

The other half of this ridiculous argument is that you take money from the mutual fund that is performing the best in your retirement plan and then you invest in the asset class or mutual fund option that is doing the worst over the previous period.

I am not making this game up. That is the basic premise of periodic or automatic rebalancing. This game would not make sense to the kids in my daughter's second grade class. But it has often passed for investment management in retirement plans.

✓ DIVERSIFICATION

I think the origin of this investment concept comes from the guy who said, "I want to be sick when I die."

Again, I will appeal to your common sense here. Why in the world would you want to be 65% invested in the asset classes and mutual funds in those asset classes that clearly have not performed well in the recent past, and have no hope of beginning to outperform after you own them? That's what a diversification strategy would suggest.

Remember that the Lifecycle mutual fund and the asset allocation pie chart use past performance data. That information is of no help to you whatsoever in the present and future management of your retirement plan account.

The financial experts who write and talk about diversification don't use the tools that you are now aware of that clearly show what stock market asset classes are over performing and underperforming. Part of the supposed investment discipline of diversification is that you should not be too heavily invested in one asset class because over time another asset class will begin to outperform.

Really? Someone should invent an investment tool that would allow a stock market investor to be able to measure the performance of mutual fund asset classes versus a benchmark--say, the S&P 500. This tool would then be able to tell you, and even show you a picture, of when one asset class is beginning to under perform, and another asset class is beginning to outperform.

And one more thing, this investment tool should have absolutely no bias or conflict of interest whatsoever. The measurement of this investment tool should just report the true performance numbers, with no opinions, predictions or commentary to confuse the issue.

See Chapters Eight and Nine for the above-mentioned investment tool. And then tell someone who is "diversified" about it. And try not to laugh at them during your explanation of Relative Strength.

Last comes the biggest financial media-induced misconception of our lifetime. You probably know what it is, but I am going to say it anyway. If it would not be for the promotion of the continued use of the following financial concept, half of the people in the financial advice industry would not be employed.

✓   ASSET ALLOCATION

Asset allocation is a little bit like diversification. They are either married to cousins or are cousins, I always forget. Asset allocation is said to have more academic credentials than diversification. You would not realize that when you try to work with asset allocation in the real investment world. In that world, asset allocation makes no investment sense.

Let me first give you my theory on asset allocation. I think it is an investment management concept that has been invented by the financial planning community in order to give them something to talk about with clients. The concept certainly does not add any investment management value as to how you should manage your retirement plan account.

Many marketing presentations throughout the 1990's claimed that asset allocation policy was by far the most important decision in investing. This concept is the main investment management concept in the current generation of on-line retirement plan investment advice tools.

The financial planner's simple recipe for investment success in the management of your retirement plan account would be for you to establish a policy of allocation to stocks, bonds and cash, and stick with it regardless of economic developments and changing asset class investment opportunities.

Consultants sell databases of historical stock market and asset class returns to financial planners. The idea is that you can take the historic numbers and put them into investment portfolio optimizers and use the result to make both current and future investment decisions.

I am sorry, but I cannot fully explain what an investment portfolio optimizer is. You know me well enough by now that if I could explain it to you, I would.

In the end, the portfolio optimizer spits out how much tolerance for risk you should have with your retirement plan account based on your number of working years until retirement, and comes up with your retirement plan investment policy.

Oh yeah, one more thing. When times get tough in the stock market like they do every few years, the financial planner tells the retirement plan investor to stick with the asset allocation policy.

With asset allocation, there is no need for the financial planner (or the retirement plan participant) to make sense of economic developments, outside stock market events like wars, or to adjust retirement plan portfolios in response to changing stock market conditions.

I think the best part of asset allocation, for those that use it, is they never have to accept responsibility for the retirement plan account portfolio performance. It is never the fault of asset allocation; it is always the stock market's fault.

The asset allocation crowd will always fight back with the fact that stock market timing does not work. And I would agree with them. I would also add that stock market timing has not one thing to do with the use of the Point & Figure risk-management tools.

Investment management should be organized around asset allocation as practiced through a filter that shows an investor an unbiased measurement of what asset classes and types of mutual funds are underperforming or outperforming the established benchmark. That again, is the concept of Relative Strength.

The idea that asset allocation will keep a retirement plan investor in the correct percentage of asset classes and individual mutual funds that are consistent with a retirement plan investor's tolerance for stock market risk is a good theory. The only problem is that it is only a theory, because it does not work in practice.

Asset allocation is offered to most retirement plan investors through the available on-line investment tools from retirement plan providers. One of the major selling points of the use of Asset Allocation is that it will help investors "sleep at night" and "stay the course" when the stock market or the mutual fund the retirement plan investor owns is going down in value--just like the period in the stock market from March 2000 through October 2002.

The most basic problem with the use of asset allocation is that the retirement plan participant is under the illusion that there is some kind of risk-management going on in her retirement plan account. But, that is not the case at all. That is never the case with the use of asset allocation.

And that is the reason that in certain stock market cycles, there is absolutely no reason a retirement plan investor should stick with a buy-and-hold-and-everything-will-be-alright investment management posture.

That is not the reality of the history of stock market investment returns. It never has been and it never will be.

Computer-generated, buy-and-hold asset allocation is inferior to real-time, unbiased and forward-looking investment management. The allocation of the monies in your retirement plan account should change in reaction to the risk conditions in the stock market. I happen to think that Bullish Percents and Relative Strength are the most important tools to use to make those changes.

YOU CAN DO BETTER THAN ASSET ALLOCATION NOW

The Internet infrastructure and database processing power to monitor stock market risk level changes is available. And it can be customized for your use with the menu of options available in your retirement plan.

You now have the two most important things you need to go forth and make better investment decisions in your retirement plan account.

First, you have the knowledge that there are tools available that will help you make better investment decisions. And with that knowledge, you should gain the confidence to make those investment decisions when the decisions have to be made.

Second, you now have the opportunity to manage your retirement plan account on your own, or work with an advisor who knows how to use the stock market risk-management tools described in this book.

CHAPTER twelve
How to Give Retirement Plan Advice

The information provided in this chapter is mainly for the investment professionals that want to build a part of their advisory practice around the retirement plan advice product. So be forewarned: the content of this chapter may, at times, get a little technical.

For the individual investors that are reading this book, there will be good information here as well. In fact, you could use this chapter as a roadmap on how to proceed with the self-direction of your retirement account.

LEARNING HOW TO WORK WITHIN THE SYSTEM

Your retirement plan offering truly is a system, an entity, even an ecosystem unto itself. Maybe I can help you with some ideas on how to survive and prosper there.

You would naturally think that if you had a question, problem or concern with your company retirement plan, you would contact your Human Resources Department or Employee Benefits Department at your company.

This would be the wrong answer. This makes too much sense to conclude that these individuals know the ins-and-outs of the company retirement plan, and that these same individuals are there to help you, as a retirement plan participant.

Unfortunately, you will find the same thing if you called the 800 number or made a visit to the retirement plan provider Web site available to you as a retirement plan participant. These people, as well as the people in your own company, are not well-versed in what is available to you as a retirement plan participant.

When your company signs up with a retirement plan provider, they sign up for a certain level of services. That includes on-line access to accounts, retirement planning tools, a menu of mutual fund options, a self-directed brokerage option, etc. Basically, your company wants to spend a certain amount of money providing a company retirement plan to employees. And the retirement plan provider wants to provide a certain level of options and services.

You, as a retirement plan participant, are stuck in the middle. This example reminds me of that great quote from one of the early NASA astronauts. He was asked when he returned to earth from space, what was going through his mind when his spaceship was hurling to earth at hundreds of miles per hour through re-entry, when there was a chance that his spaceship would blow up if there was a problem.

The astronaut said he was thinking about the fact that the parts on his spaceship were all provided to NASA--like any government agency-- by the lowest bidder.

Well, ladies and gentlemen retirement plan participants, you are in the same situation. The company that provides your retirement plan is not going to provide one more thing than what is currently on the service level that is included in your company retirement plan.

When you add to that some of the legendary stories of how cheap and uncaring many retirement plan sponsors are, then you have an idea of what you are working with to try to find even the most basic help with information on your retirement plan offerings.

But that does not mean I am not going to try to help. I know as much of the tricks and tips as anyone that will take the time to type this information onto a computer screen.

My advice would be to leave the retirement plan sponsor out of the equation. That, again, would be your Human Resources or Employee Benefits people at the retirement plan sponsor. They just don't understand and don't want to understand any more than the basics of the retirement plan offerings.

FOCUS YOUR EFFORTS ON THE RETIREMENT PLAN PROVIDER

Instead, I would focus my attention on the retirement plan provider. Like a lot of things in business, the company that has the money (and in this case, your retirement money) is the one you have to focus on.

Your company (the retirement plan sponsor), has contracted for a defined level of options in your company retirement plan and a defined level of services available in your company retirement plan. Each company retirement plan is different, so I can't get into many details or specifics here. But there are some things that you should know about that are common to all retirement plans.

Take, as an example, the subject of paying third-party advisory fees out of the retirement plan participant account. The retirement plan document that your retirement plan sponsor (your company) signs, will not prevent a retirement plan participant from paying fees to a third-party. But I will guarantee you that if you bring that issue up with anyone in your Human Resources or Employee Benefits Department; they will tell you flat-out that it can not be done.

It can be done. My firm does it all the time, and with companies that are members of the Fortune 500.

If you run into a roadblock in your attempt to get advisory fees paid to a third-party advisor, focus on the retirement plan provider. That is the entity in the equation that has to make the process available.

Now I want to give you a little more ammunition for any potential battle you may have with our retirement plan provider. There is no law on the books at the Department of Labor or at the Internal Revenue Service that says you can't use your retirement plan account to pay for third-party advice. And don't ever let anyone tell you that there is.

The ability to pay for third-party investment advice from your retirement plan balance is a decision that can be made by the retirement plan provider. In my experience, the only way that can happen is if you, or a group of your retirement plan co-participants, ask for the option to be made available.

I have had conversations with several of the large retirement plan providers about this issue. I have never been told that a third-party fee payment is unavailable. But the retirement plan provider has to somehow be motivated to make this feature available.

SELF-DIRECTED RETIREMENT ACCOUNT OPTION

First, let me define a couple of retirement plan terms. All retirement plans offered to retirement plan participants are called "participant directed plans." That means that each participant can direct the monies in his or her retirement plan into any of the menu of options available in the retirement plan.

A "self-directed retirement plan" is different. That means that in addition to the menu of mutual fund options available to retirement plan participants (the default menu), there is the ability to "self-direct." Self-direction means that the retirement plan participant can move all or part of her retirement plan account balance off of the main menu of mutual fund options.

In my retirement plan advisory work, I have run into two main types of self-directed retirement plan options. First, a retirement plan participant would have the ability to invest in an expanded menu of mutual funds options in a self-directed retirement plan. So instead of eight to twelve mutual fund options on the default retirement plan menu, the self-directed retirement plan investor would have as many as 2,500 mutual fund choices available to her.

Obviously, this opens up a whole new world to a retirement plan participant. The most important changes here are that retirement plan investors can dramatically upgrade the quality of the mutual fund options in their retirement plans.

As an example, if there is only one good Small Cap Value mutual fund option in the default retirement plan menu, in a self-directed retirement plan menu, there would be 35 to 40 good Small Cap mutual fund options.

These expanded choices are especially important in the area of specialty mutual funds options, such as natural resources, gold, real estate, etc. Just like those same sectors in the stock market, these specialized mutual funds can have dramatic runs upward at certain times in the stock market cycle.

In addition, the expanded menu of mutual fund options available to a self-directed retirement plan investor includes the Inverse Market Mutual Funds. These are mutual funds that go up in value as the stock market indices decline in price.

Let me repeat that last bit of information, because I know from experience that retirement plan investors that hear that information for the first time often need it repeated.

There are mutual funds available that go up in value as the major U.S. stock market indices---S&P 500, NASDAQ 100---go down in value. There are even mutual funds that go up in value as interest rates rise.

Used with the stock market risk-management tools that you are now aware of, the self-directed brokerage option can be a very valuable retirement plan offering to retirement plan investors, or to retirement plan investors who work with advisors to help them navigate the self-directed brokerage environment.

The costs for this self-directed brokerage option vary. I have seen the annual costs vary anywhere from $25 to $200 per year.

SELF-DIRECTED OPTION THAT IS TOTALLY SELF-DIRECTED

The second type of self-directed brokerage option is not nearly as common, but it is something worth mentioning. That is, the ability to move off of the default mutual fund menu in a retirement plan and into a self-directed brokerage option that includes the ability to buy common stocks.

In this environment, the retirement plan participant is not limited to a menu of no-load mutual funds. The retirement plan participant can buy any stock, bond or mutual fund available to a U.S. investor.

Again, this totally self-directed retirement plan offering is not widely available. The retirement plan sponsors that mainly use this are law firms, doctors groups, and some professional organizations.

Finally, the totally self-directed retirement plan offering does increase the costs to the retirement plan participant, often dramatically. There are buying and selling transaction costs associated with these types of accounts just like with the typical brokerage account.

PAYING FOR ADVICE

Another feature of self-directed brokerage accounts is probably the most important recent development in the retirement plan industry. This feature is still not widely available, but I find it is becoming more readily available. That is the ability to pay a third-party investment advisor fees with dollars from the retirement plan account.

The ability of retirement plan participants to pay for help making the right investment decisions in the management of their retirement plans is a big selling point to my advisory work. If you think about the convenience of this feature and the fact that the retirement plan participant does not have to physically write a check every quarter to receive retirement plan advice, it does make a huge difference.

Just look at the mathematics of the savings. For example, let's say my firm charges a retirement plan participant $250 per quarter, or $1000 per year to provide advice on the menu of options available in her retirement plan. In order to have the $1000 available to pay my fees, the retirement plan participant would have to earn $1,666.67 in income to net

$1000 to pay me. That calculation assumes a 40% state and federal tax bracket, which I am sure to any reader of this book, a reasonable position.

The ability to pay my firm the $1000 every year from the retirement plan account is a money-saving and time-saving proposition--especially when the help making the right investment decisions in the retirement plan account is factored in.

From my experience, the ability to pay advisory fees to a third-party investment advisor from a retirement plan account balance is not a universal offering. It is, however, much easier to accomplish when a self-directed brokerage account is involved in the retirement plan menu.

Most large retirement plan provider firms are not in the brokerage account business. They do not want to go through the expense of providing these services to their retirement plan participants. So they "farm out" the business to discount brokerage firms like Ameritrade, Schwab and Fidelity.

HOW TO MANAGE WHAT YOU HAVE AVAILABLE

Once you figure out your menu of available retirement plan options and if you can easily pay to get help, and then you have to know how to manage your retirement plan menu options. That is what we are going to discuss now.

Don't rely on your quarterly account statement from your retirement plan provider for the following information. Remember that they only do what is necessary, not necessarily what is right. Go on-line to your retirement plan provider Web site and get a list of all of the available options in your retirement plan menu.

For most of the readers here, that will be a menu of options from 8 to 25 mutual funds. For the retirement plan participants that have a self-directed brokerage account option available to them, that may be 3,000. We will solve that problem in a minute.

Each mutual fund option available in your retirement plan menu will have what is called a "ticker symbol". The ticker symbol is a 5-letter code that always ends with an X. As an example, the ticker symbol for the Fidelity Magellan Fund is FMAGX. The ticker symbol is used to look up the price of the mutual fund on the national stock, bond and mutual fund quote systems that are available to investors.

THE ANNUITY SUB-ACCOUNT SITUATION

There are some exceptions here. And the first one would be if your retirement plan sponsor uses an annuity as your retirement plan offering. In an annuity, there is an entity called a "sub-account." Most annuity sub-accounts do not have ticker symbols. That is, they do not have a publicly-traded forum that allows you to follow the price of the security on a daily basis.

After all, why would your company or your company's retirement plan provider, want you to be able to easily follow what is going on with your retirement plan money? That would be too easy.

What you have to do in this case is not a pretty scene. You have to call the 800 number for your company retirement plan provider and ask the recently-graduated-from-college person on the other end of the phone the following question.

A special note here: you will be able to tell that the person you are talking to is a recent college graduate by the way he reacts to this question. That is because no one has ever asked him this question before. And in his training, he was taught what he should say if anyone ever dared to ask him this question.

Here is the question:

> *"What are the publicly-traded mutual fund ticker symbols that correspond to the menu of mutual fund options available in my retirement plans?"*

Here is the answer, right out of the employee training manual and the role-playing exercises in the employee training class:

> *"The sub-accounts in your retirement menu are not publicly-traded. They have no ticker symbol."*

I should confess one thing here: you will only get the response you see above if the person you ask the question even knows what a ticker symbol is.

At this point, you have to ask for a Supervisor on the 800 number help desk. There is no amount of education that you can give this person that will allow them to understand what you need. And the fact is, as a retirement plan participant, you are entitled to this information!

Tell the supervisor that you know that the sub-accounts in your retirement plan do not have ticker symbols. But every mutual fund that is offered in an annuity sub-account has a ticker symbol. Or the sub-account follows an industry index like the S&P 500 or the Russell 3000.

WHAT TO DO AFTER YOU FIND WHAT YOU HAVE

After you gather up all of the names and ticker symbols of the mutual fund options available in your retirement plan, you need to look for a place to manage all of the information that you need to make better decisions.

I want to say a couple of things to those lucky individuals that have a self-directed option available to them on their retirement plan menu. First, your really need a place to keep all of the ticker symbols in order. You will be overwhelmed by the number of mutual fund options available at the custodian firms---Ameritrade, Schwab, and Fidelity---for self-directed retirement plan accounts. I have seen a minimum of 300 options all the way up to 2,500 options.

Secondly, don't be intimidated by this number of options available to you. There are mutual fund databases available that manage this kind of information. And they don't cost much to buy (under $100 or on a monthly basis $15-$25 per month). These costs are well worth the money. Especially when you see the returns in your retirement plan account begin to improve dramatically.

WHAT THE PROS USE...DORSEY WRIGHT AND ASSOCIATES INC.

This is as good a time as any to pause for a station break. This is not really a commercial. You can't write a commercial for the investment research firm that changed not only your business and your life, but the lives of your clients as well.

Dorsey, Wright & Associates, Inc. is based in Richmond, Virginia. For 18 years they have provided Point & Figure research and provided the training and database to use that research. The stock, bond and mutual fund information they provide is available to both professional investment advisors as well as serious individual investors.

Dorsey, Wright and Associates, Inc.
1-800-247-5234.
www.DorseyWright.com

I can't speak to building a retirement plan advisory business using anything better than the tools and information on the Dorsey, Wright Web site. I have never done it. And even after 21 years in this business, I don't know of any other tools or resources that would allow it to be done.

OTHER RETIREMENT PLANNING TOOLS

There are other databases that allow you to enter the ticker symbols of the mutual fund options available in your retirement plan menu, and then manage that information, but you have to be careful. These are the same type of databases that are now commonly offered by the retirement plan providers.

If you want to look take the time necessary to answer investment questionnaires about your age, when you want to retire, and how much risk you want to take with your retirement plan money, there is a lot of free information available on the Internet. The more sophisticated retirement plan tool providers can even tell you how much money you should have at your expected retirement date

The operative word in that explanation is FREE. I suppose I should ask the obvious question here in case someone is not paying attention to the intended message here. "What is the value of FREE information?" It is certainly not valuable enough to use to make decisions with your retirement plan money.

It has been my experience that the free information available is not much different that the tools available at the larger retirement plan providers. I am sure you have seen these offerings when you have had the time to log on to your retirement plan provider Web site.

The retirement plan provider industry has figured out a few things in recent years. One is that there is not much utilization of the on-line tools currently available to retirement plan participants. Depending on what trade magazine you read, and who is quoted in the article, the reasons for the low levels of use are the obvious ones.

First, what retirement plan participant has the time and energy necessary to go on-line and fill out a bunch of personal information, and get back a series of recommendations that they don't understand?

Second, for those few brave souls that did at one time go on-line, sit through the procedure, and use the recommendations to structure their retirement plan portfolio, how have they performed? Are they retired yet?

The multi-colored pie charts that are created for you spit out the optimal mix of mutual funds in your retirement plan menu that you should own. Right now. So these tools at least tell you what to do in your retirement plan with the money you have there now.

It is at the exact second that you click on the Log Off button on your retirement plan provider Web site that the trouble begins with these on-line retirement plan tools.

As you drive home from work this evening, or as you drove into work this morning, did you make decisions based on how your driving circumstances changed? Did those changes allow you to arrive at your destination safely and soundly? Great. The reason your driving was successful was that you made those changes as your driving conditions changed.

The problem with any on-line retirement plan investment tools, and with any computer-generated asset allocation investment software, is that it does not make changes in your investments when the conditions in the stock market change.

We talked before about the importance of your age when you fill in the information necessary to generate a risk-management profile from one of these on-line retirement planning sources. Your age is one of only two variables these programs use to advise you to make changes in your retirement plan investment strategy.

The theory is that as you get older, you need to become more conservative with your investment strategy. Translated, you need to own less stock and more bonds as you get older.

The other major piece of information used by the computer-generated on-line retirement plan tools is the anniversary of when you completed your data input. There is no special reason for this, other than the fact that the computer needs to file the information as of a certain date.

On the anniversary of your account, you will be notified that it is time for you to "rebalance" your asset allocation in your retirement plan. That means it is time for you to review how you have done with how the computer has told you to invest.

At that time, you will be told to make the following moves in your retirement plan. First, you sell a percentage of the mutual funds that you owned over the last year that outperformed the stock market benchmark. Second, you take the money from the sale of the mutual funds that performed well, and you buy more shares of the mutual funds you own that did not do well at all in the last year.

Yes, you read these instructions correctly. You sell part of the mutual funds in your retirement plan that did well in the past year. Common sense would tell you that maybe you should own more of these mutual funds going forward, but you have to remember here that this recommendation is coming to you from a computer.

The above procedure is called "rebalancing." We discussed it in detail in Chapter Eleven. There is no other logical explanation for the process of "rebalancing" your retirement plan account based on some arbitrary date that has nothing to do with the current risk level of the stock market. And based on some useless concept that calculates the relationship of your age and your need to own less stocks as you get older.

If I tried to sell you on the logic of the concept of "rebalancing" your retirement plan account every year, there is no way you would allow it to happen. Yet because this same concept comes from a computer that knows how old you are, and how much risk you said you want to take in your retirement plan investing, retirement plan investors allow it to happen to them all of the time.

There is no mention made as to why you should be invested in those specific mutual funds, and in those percentages in your account. The only thing I have been able to figure out when I have tried to use those retirement plan tools is that most of the calculations are based on your current age and when you want to retire. That is the only way I have been able to change the investment percentages and the mutual fund recommendations.

If these on-line retirement plan asset-allocation tools worked, even a little bit, I would not have felt compelled to write this book. If I had met one retirement plan participant that had the time to use these on-line tools, follow the recommended asset allocation, get back to daily life and be successful in this buy-and-hold investment management posture, I would say so.

This on-line retirement plan investment advice stuff does not work. If it is offered by your retirement plan provider, or you come across it on the Internet, the fact is, it still does not work. Even if you took the same information, and hired an investment advisor that followed the detailed recommendations and made the investment changes for you, it still would not work. And it would not have worked in the past.

What is needed is an active, real-time set of stock market risk-management tools. These tools have to be adaptable to the constant changes in the stock market. They have to be grounded in common sense economic principles in order to give users the timely information necessary to manage their retirement plans according to how things actually are in the stock markets, as compared to how the financial media says things are in the stock markets.

Last, they have to be easy-to-use. So easy, that they give users the confidence to set up their retirement plan portfolio based on the level of risk they are willing to accept. And then go back when the stock market changes, and make the necessary adjustments to lessen the risk, or increase the risk--when the opportunity arises.

CONCLUSION

I hope I have succeeded in my objective to better educate and expose you to the stock market risk-management tools available today. You are now armed with all of the information and resources necessary to accomplish the three great goals in the management of your retirement plan account:

1. Protect your retirement plan account from unnecessary stock market losses.

2. At times, reduce the amount of stock market risk you take by moving a portion of your retirement account to the safety of the money market.

3. Improve the long-term investment performance of your retirement plan account.

You have been exposed to all the necessary stock market risk-management tools. You now have the ability to know when you grow the value of your retirement plan account. And you now know when you have to work to preserve the value of your retirement plan account. Said another way, you now can be aggressively invested in the stock market when prices are generally rising, and defensive in your stock market investing in the early stages of a stock market decline.

With this new set of investment tools, comes a new set of investment management rights to you as a retirement plan participant. Now you don't have to settle for the same investment returns as other participants in your company retirement plan. I urge you to take advantage of your new rights as soon as you can. Whether you choose to do-it-yourself, or work with an experienced advisor who has the same stock market investment principles as you do, get started on your new stock market risk plan.

Last, learn to deal with the facts in the stock markets and not the perceptions. Don't listen to anyone's opinion on the direction of the stock market—including your own. You now have knowledge and access to the investment management tools that can really help you pay attention to what is happening in the stock markets. And that is the first step on the road to being a more disciplined and intelligent stock market investor.

CHART AND TABLE EXAMPLES

All charts and tables courtesy of Dorsey Wright and Associates

Gaps in Investment Performance

Hide Returns |Printable| Bell Curve

* Restrictions may apply

Click the Heading to Sort	Symbol	Desc	Category	Class	7 Day	30 Day	YTD	1Year	Trend	RS	RS Col	Score *	Date
Large Cap Funds	RMFEX	Amer Funds Amer Mut R4	Growth & Income	All Large Cap⬜ Value	0.1	1.5	4.3	8.1	P	B	O	4.4+	Click
	QUAGX	Quaker Strategic Gr A	Aggressive Growth	All Large Cap Groth	-0.3	-0.3	2.1	11.6	P	S	O	3.3	Click
	AGTHX	Amer Funds Grth Fund A	Growth-Domestic	All Large Cap Growth	-0.7	1.5	2.0	13.3	P	S	O	3.2+	Click
Small Cap Funds	SCUIX	Schroder US Opport Inv	Small Cap	All Small Cap Growth	-1.6	-0.3	8.2	13.6	P	B	X	5.2	Click
	AVPAX	American Beacon SmCV1Pn	Small Cap	All Small Cap⬜ Value	-1.6	-0.3	3.7	6.3	P	B	X	4.7-	Click
Global Funds	REREX	Amer Funds EuroPac R4	Non-US Equity	All Large Cap Blend	-0.3	2.6	6.5	27.5	P	B	X	5.3+	Click
	REOIX	Laudus Rosenberg IntlEqInstl	Non-US Equity	All Large Cap Value	-0.2	1.9	8.9	26.1	P	B	X	4.9-	Click
Fixed Income Funds	PMTAX	PIMCO Total Ret Mtg Adm	General Mortgage	N/A	-0.1	-0.3	-1.9	-3.5	P	S	O	1.7	Click
	BHYSX	BlackRock High Yld Bd Svc	Corp Bond High Yield	All Small Cap Value	0.1	-0.6	-0.8	-1.5	N	S	O	0.6-	Click

This table shows the large gaps in investment performance among the various mutual fund retirement plan options.

- Trend: P= Positive, N=Negative
- RS (Relative Strength): O is negative, X is positive
- RS Col (Relative Strength column): O is declining, X is rising.
- Score: This column is the mutual fund's technical score as calculated on the Dorsey Wright mutual fund database. The highest possible score is 6.0 and the lowest possible score is 0.0."

Small Cap Outperforming Large Cap

```
34.008  I  I  I              34.008      ┌────────────────────────┐
31.932  I  I  I              31.932      │     S&P Small Cap       │
29.983  I  I  I              29.983      │        Verus           │
28.153  I  I  I              28.153      │   S&P 500 Large Cap     │
26.435  I _ I  A   -------   26.435      │  (X-Overweight RSP)     │
24.822  I  I  B              24.822      │  (O = Overweight SPX)   │
23.307  I  I  X              23.307      │     2-17-2000 to:       │
21.884  I  I  4              21.884      │  ┌──────────────────┐   │
20.549  7  7  1   -------   20.549      │  │ SML              │   │
19.294  X  O  8   -------   19.294      │  │ SPX              │   │
18.117  X  O  6   -------   18.117      └────────────────────────┘
17.011  I  6  2              17.011
15.973  I  7  3              15.973
14.998  I  8  2              14.998
14.083  I  A  X              14.083
13.223  I  2  X  ◄═ 2/17/02 ═ .223
12.416  I  3  I              12.416
11.658  I  I  I              11.658
10.947  I  I  I              10.947
10.279  I  I  I              10.279
 9.651  I  I  I               9.651
 9.062  I  I  I               9.062
```

Shown is the reversal up in the SML (S&P 600 Small Cap Index) versus the S&P 500 Index on 2-17-2000. This was the specific date that the Small Cap stock index began to "outperform" the Large Cap stock index (SPX).

Tables Showing Gaps in Performance

Fidelity Magellan

	Curr Value	0/24/200 to 01/01/2006		YTD	
		$ Change	% Change	$ Change	% Change
FMAGX	86.33	$-12.47	-12.65%	$0.2230	0.2590%
MDY	137.75	$53.57	66.03%	$3.06	2.27%
SML	369.78	$152.57	77.72%	$19.11	5.45%
S&P 500 Equal Weight	1693.93	$513.23	44.07%	$34.84	2.10%
S&P 500	1265.48	$-220.97	-15.04%	$17.19	1.38%
Dow Jones	11090.67	$-779.60	-6.78%	$373.17	3.48%
NASDAQ	2130.06	$-1863.88	-45.80%	$-75.26	-3.41%

The returns for Indices, ETFs and Stocks do not reflect dividends

Performance of the Fidelity Magellan fund versus the MDY (S&P 400 Mid Cap Index) and the SML (S&P 600 Small Cap Index) over the 1-1-2000 to the 1-1-2006 time period.

Fidelity Magellan is one of the most popular mutual funds in 401(k) retirement plan menus.

Amer Funds Grth Fund A

	Curr Value	0/24/200 to 01/01/2006		YTD	
		$ Change	% Change	$ Change	% Change
AGTHX	31.47	$6.16	24.95%	$0.6100	1.9767%
MDY	137.75	$53.57	66.03%	$3.06	2.27%
SML	369.78	$152.57	77.72%	$19.11	5.45%
S&P 500 Equal Weight	1693.93	$513.23	44.07%	$34.84	2.10%
S&P 500	1265.48	$-220.97	-15.04%	$17.19	1.38%
Dow Jones	11090.67	$-779.60	-6.78%	$373.17	3.48%
NASDAQ	2130.06	$-1863.88	-45.80%	$-75.26	-3.41%

The returns for Indices, ETFs and Stocks do not reflect dividends

American Funds Growth Fund of America over the same time period as Magellan (above).

This fund is also one of the most popular 401(k) retirement plan options.

PIMCO Total Ret Instl

	Curr Value	0/24/200 to 01/01/2006		YTD	
		$ Change	% Change	$ Change	% Change
PTTRX	10.18	$1.70	19.47%	$-0.2750	-2.6303%
MDY	137.75	$53.57	66.03%	$3.06	2.27%
SML	369.78	$152.57	77.72%	$19.11	5.45%
S&P 500 Equal Weight	1693.93	$513.23	44.07%	$34.84	2.10%
S&P 500	1265.48	$-220.97	-15.04%	$17.19	1.38%
Dow Jones	11090.67	$-779.60	-6.78%	$373.17	3.48%
NASDAQ	2130.06	$-1863.88	-45.80%	$-75.26	-3.41%

The returns for Indices, ETFs and Stocks do not reflect dividends

This chart is used to illustrate the same performance concept as the Fidelity Magellan and American Funds Growth Fund of America. The PIMCO Total Return Fund is the most popular bond fund investment option in 401(k) retirement plan menus.

S&P Mid-Cap 400 SPDRs

	Curr Value	0/24/200 to 01/01/2006		YTD	
		$ Change	% Change	$ Change	% Change
MDY	137.75	$51.82	62.52%	$3.06	2.27%
S&P 500 Equal Weight	1693.93	$636.99	62.32%	$34.84	2.10%
S&P 500	1265.48	$-105.13	-7.77%	$17.19	1.38%
Dow Jones	11090.67	$624.90	6.19%	$373.17	3.48%
NASDAQ	2130.06	$-2412.08	-52.24%	$-75.26	-3.41%

The returns for Indices, ETFs and Stocks do not reflect dividends

Large performance gap between the MDY (S&P Mid Cap 400 Index) and the S&P 500 Index over the 2-24-2000 to 1-1-2006 time period.

S&P 600 Small Cap Index

	Curr Value	0/24/200 to 01/01/2006		YTD	
		$ Change	% Change	$ Change	% Change
MDY	369.78	$146.46	7172%	$19.11	5.45%
S&P 500 Equal Weight	1693.93	$592.47	55.55%	$34.84	2.10%
S&P 500	1265.48	$-168.55	-11.90%	$17.19	1.38%
Dow Jones	11090.67	$73.90	0.69%	$373.17	3.48%
NASDAQ	2130.06	$-2280.28	-50.84%	$-75.26	-3.41%

The returns for Indices, ETFs and Stocks do not reflect dividends

Large performance gap between the SML (S&P 600 Small Cap Index) and the S&P 500 Index over the 2-10-2000 to 1-1-2006 time period.

2821240

Made in the USA